A Hidden Fire

A Hidden Fire

Exploring the deeper reaches of prayer

Brother Ramon SSF

Marshall Pickering

Marshall Morgan and Scott
Marshall Pickering
3 Beggarwood Lane, Basingstoke, Hants RG23 7LP, UK

First published as a pocket paperback in 1985 by
Marshall Morgan and Scott Publications Ltd
Part of the Marshall Pickering Holdings Group
A subsidiary of the Zondervan Corporation
Re-issued in this larger format 1987

Reprinted:Impression number
87 88 89   5432

British Library Cataloguing in Publication Data

Ramon, Brother, S.S.F.
   A hidden fire: exploring the deeper reaches of prayer.
   1. Prayer
   I. Title
   248.3'2   BV215

ISBN 0 551 01247 1

Printed in Great Britain by
The Guernsey Press Co. Ltd., Guernsey, Channel Islands.

For David and Edna,
my father and mother,
in gratitude
and love

Contents

Foreword

Ramon and I have known many times of deep Christian fellowship through the years since we were together in College. In those days we shared an accordian – loaned to us by our music teacher – and paid for one lesson a week that we shared. Since then our paths have diverged and crossed many times. As his ability on the accordian, so has his pilgrimage been – much richer and fuller than mine.

The first section of his book helpfully sets the scene auto-biographically. From it can be gathered the nature of his spirituality. Some will not want to read on – theirs will be the loss. Others will long for the deep sense of the reality of the presence of God about which he writes. In sections two and three that follow, there is so much to enlighten, so much to inspire and so much to provoke thoughtful questions.

This is not a book for the spiritually timid, nor for those bound by the chains of their own tradition. Ramon is Catholic. His evangelical and charismatic experience, woven into his sacramental and Catholic, not to say Orthodox spirituality make for a practical manual on prayer and the great spiritual traditions, full of information and insight.

What he writes will inspire deeper devotion; it will make the reader covet his genuine spirituality.

Through it Ramon conveys his real concern to help people learn *HOW* to pray.

Peter D Manson
Pentecost 1985

Prologue: A Hidden Fire

It isn't easy to keep a fire hidden, and it is the paradox of the fire of God that it is both hidden and manifest. The fire which burned upon the holy altar of God was never to be extinguished: 'Fire shall be kept burning upon the altar continually; it shall not go out.'[1] It symbolises the fire of the divine Love and the divine Holiness of which Charles Wesley writes:

> O Thou who camest from above
> The pure celestial fire to impart,
> Kindle a flame of sacred love
> On the mean altar of my heart.

It is a fire that belongs to God. It burns upon God's altar in his most holy temple. We are the temple of God, and our inmost heart is the altar of the living God. As John Chrysostom says: 'No matter where we happen to be, by prayer we set up an altar to God in our hearts.' James Montgomery speaks of this hiddenness in his hymn on the many aspects of prayer:

> Prayer is the soul's sincere desire,
> Uttered or unexpressed;
> The motion of a hidden fire
> That trembles in the breast.

This book is concerned with the hidden life of prayer. But if this hidden fire truly burns, it will communicate and manifest itself in the quality of life, it will burn with both radiance and fierce heat, with gentle warmth and with mighty burnings.

11

When the desert bush burned in a mighty conflagration and yet was not consumed, Moses turned aside to see such a great thing – and suddenly he was face to face with the Living God.[2] The Psalmist tried to keep the inward fire hidden and smothered, but it was impossible: '. . . my distress grew worse, my heart became hot within me. As I mused the fire burned . . .'[3] Jeremiah tried to quench the holy flame, by not speaking the word of the Lord which burned within him, but an impossible situation developed: 'If I say, "I will not mention him, or speak any more in his name, there is in my heart as it were a burning fire shut up in my bones, and I am weary with holding it in, and I cannot." '[4]

It is this inward flame, this scorching fire of love and holiness with which we are concerned. It is the communication of the secret, inward, hidden fire which burns within, and communicates by its very nature.

But words are dangerous. The communcation of the divine fire is not in words alone; words in themselves may be the outward profession of something which has not become an inward possession. Thomas Merton makes the point that reading of a truth, a doctrine or a spiritual experience sometimes causes the reader to *imagine* that he is in possession of the matter spoken of. 'The letter kills,' says the apostle, 'but the Spirit gives life.'[5]

This book is a sharing not of words alone, but of spiritual experience. The life of prayer is an intensely personal thing, but it is not individualistic. It has to be personal before it can be corporate, and even the hermit with a genuine vocation to the life of solitary prayer is not alone. The prayer which summons and consumes him* is an intense and concentrated participation in the life of prayer to which every Christian is called.

As I have travelled around the country during the past

* Throughout I have tried to use language which includes both female and male. But I wish to make it clear that when I use the formal masculine pronoun, it is to be taken in a generic sense. I know more female than male hermits!

12

nine years or so as a friar, leading evangelistic or ministry missions, and conducting retreats on the life of prayer, I am faced with the same problem posed in various ways. We have a Franciscan 'Third Order' of single and married people called 'Tertiaries', many of them young married couples with children. At our Families' Camp in Dorset last year one such group said: 'We read and hear of the importance of prayer, the value of prayer, the meaning of prayer, the primacy of prayer, but no one tells us *how* to pray.'

Even as I wrote that last sentence, I was called down to our friary garden where a young family had come to see one of the brothers. As I talked with the mother she said: 'I am involved in an increasing amount of work in my local church, but I need a place, a space where I can come to pray, and someone to talk to in order to deepen my life of prayer.'

This book is a sharing of personal experiences which are part of the ongoing and dynamic life of the Church. I am well aware of the deadness, the archaic structures, the lack of vital holiness and gospel love which marks so many parts of the Church. But I must affirm that I have learned to live and love and grow within the fellowship of believing Christians. Some of them are Catholics (of the Roman and Anglican variety), some are Orthodox (of the Eastern variety), and some are Evangelicals and Pentecostals (of all varieties). God does not seem as interested as we are in our labels, and perhaps it is because I have a spiritual home in the Anglican tradition, with gratitude for an evangelical and pentecostal experience, that I feel a certain inward freedom which I long to share.

The first section of this book, EXPERIENCE, traces my own process of spiritual development from childhood up to the present time, with both tremendous joy and darkness involved. The second section, EXPERIMENT, includes teaching and practice to involve the reader in practical methods of experimentation. It is not only the *what* and the *why* of prayer, but considers the *how* question!

The third section, EXPOSURE, deals with the classic way of prayer, the deeper reaches of the life of prayer, a path open to all Christians, but actually travelled by so few. It is exposure to the light and life and love of the mystery we call God, and the transfiguration which takes place in such exposure and confrontation, leading at last to union with him.

It is my prayer that we shall all enter more profoundly into a living experience, described in the opening chapters of the Acts of the Apostles: 'And there appeared to them tongues as of fire, distributed and resting on each one of them. And they were all filled with the Holy Spirit . . .'[6]

References

1 Leviticus 6:13
2 Exodus 31:6
3 Psalm 39:2,3
4 Jeremiah 23:29
5 2 Corinthians 3:6
6 Acts 2:3f

Brother Ramon SSF,
The Society of Saint Francis,
September 1985

Part I: Experience

1: Prayer: An Experience of the Holy Trinity

God the Father

My first recollection of the experience of God is one of wonder and joy, at about seven years of age. Long before that, indeed ever since I can remember, I was aware of a sense of mystery which often touched my life. I could not describe or interpret this awareness, because it arose from intuitive childhood depths which have no theological language or thought forms to explain them. The recollection referred to above was given to me as I sat alone one night upon a low, brick wall. The stars were shining in the spaciousness of high sky and darkness. The immensity gave way to wonder and joy, as I felt embraced by a love beyond anything I had known.

I recollect and interpret *now* the immediacy of the experience *then*. It is one of those 'staying' experiences which orientated my life towards basic wonder and joy, which remain constant as the chapters of my life unfold. There is always danger in relating experiences of childhood, of imposing more mature concepts upon the primitive immediacy of the child's heart and mind. I would not then have been able either to think about, much less communicate, an understanding of the twin doctrines of the transcendence and the immanence of God – the God who is above and beyond anything we can think or imagine, and who also enters human history and our own lives. These are two ideas I may use now, to understand this experience. But I realize that even in trying to explain this experience doctrinally, I erect a barrier between the clarity of the actual experience, and its communication in later years to other people.

I come from a loving and emotionally satisfying home, and the close bonds with both parents continue to this day. But it wasn't a specifically 'religious' home. So up to about ten years of age my understanding of God was primarily what I felt and knew to be true within myself. During that first formative decade I was often alone, and went wandering and wondering along the coast of the Gower peninsula. I often felt a (sometimes overwhelming) sense of presence, of mystery, what I would later call the 'numinous'. There was a mixture of awe, wonder and yearning in this childhood experience. It was not so much a 'heavenly Father image,' in the sense of my own father's relationship to me. I did appreciate that analogy, but there was a more 'impersonal' sense of mystery than that. Let me illustrate.

One day my father was taking me across a busy thorough-fare. He said something like: 'Now keep hold of my hand tightly, because if you don't, you are likely to get run over.' I knew he was not serious in his seriousness. Of course I was to hold tightly to him, but I also knew that whether I held on or not, he would hold me. There was danger, but with him there I was kept from it by his love and strength. The impersonal nature of the mystery I had felt in the created order was not less than that – but more. It was not that my experience was of the sub-personal, but of the supra-personal.

This natural theology was communicated to me from earth and sea and sky. If I had read some of the Celtic mon-astic devotional writings and poetry at that time, they would have connected with my own experience. It was not the re-demptive experience of the Christian tradition, nor even of the Hebrew tradition (for the God of creation is the God of redemption): it was too early for that! My experience of God was of the creator-sustainer who is both transcendent above his creation in holiness and glory, and present in the very stuff of his material creation. If I had known the 104th psalm, my experience would have affirmed many of its verses:

When thou hidest thy face, they are dismayed;
When thou takest away thy breath, they die
and return to their dust.
When thou sendest forth thy Spirit, they are created;
and thou renewest the face of the ground. (vv.29,30)

God the Son

Then I began attending a Sunday School where I met people who lived what they sang and preached about! It was not long before my childhood awareness of wonder and joy was concentrated in the cross of Christ. At twelve years of age I entered into an experience of conversion in which Jesus became the Christ to me. This began a personal relationship within the fellowship of the Church which is as fresh to me now as it was then; it deepens in wonder and joy, in spite of personal and corporate pain and darkness which I shall describe later.

There were many deficiencies in the Christian teaching which I received: it made a strong division between nature and grace, and promoted a doctrine which some call 'total depravity'. This maintained that the *imago Dei*, the image of God in man, was not merely distorted or broken, but completely obliterated and destroyed. There was no continuity between God and man, no natural revelation, no manifestation of the divine in the created order for unregenerate man. This contradicted my own childhood experience. It may have been Western Augustinianism or Protestant hyper-Calvinism, but it was not the Gospel. I could never understand why sin was called 'original' when according to the Genesis story it was innocence that was original!

But be that as it may, I did enter into an inebriating love of God in the redeeming experience of Christ. The person of Jesus focused for me what had been confused mystery, and the embrace of an impersonal benevolence. Here was a human being who manifested the ways of God so clearly in his life and teaching that I became convinced that he was God manifested in the flesh. I was given orthodox teaching regarding the person and nature of Christ, and this strengthened, rather than contradicted, my previous experience.

Now, when I heard Philip's question: 'Lord, show us the Father and we shall be satisfied,' I could affirm, from my own experience Jesus' answer: 'Have I been with you so long, and yet you do not know me, Philip? He who has seen me has seen the Father.'[1] I read the New Testament avidly, especially the gospels. I remember walking down the street, repeating chapter one of St. John's first epistle, determined to learn the whole epistle by heart. I look back with great joy to those days, for I can still repeat chapters of the Authorised Version of the Bible, and catch again the thrill and joy of my 'first love' for Christ.

So it was, in my pilgrimage of prayer, that my early childhood was filled with the sense of the presence of God the Father. The innocence of childhood, of nature, and the world of the imagination was the substance of my childhood spirituality. I was aware of areas of darkness both in myself and in the world at that time, for there are none so sensitive to loneliness and pain as children who are loved and yet who love solitude. My early childhood search found fruition in the experience of conversion to faith in Christ. The time came, even at twelve years, to recognize an objective element which would guide and channel my interior spiritual search. That happened over a period of a few months prior to what I can only call an evangelical experience. I had been learning and storing up knowledge of scripture, and observing joy and enthusiasm among some of the members of the Sunday School which I had begun to attend. One Sunday evening I went along to a Missionary Service in which young people about to embark on missionary service overseas were sharing their experience of Christ and call to his service. One young woman with radiant face and glowing witness personified for me what a life surrendered to Christ could mean. Here was someone who not only knew, but could communicate what I had read concerning Jesus – and I wanted that quality of life, that assurance, that joy.

The whole theme of that service was call, challenge, decision for Christ; it was one of those rare moments when the time of decision was upon me. I felt a deep emotional surge of response which carried me forward to a simple prayer of surrender to Christ, mingled with tears of joy. Again, I could not have put it into words, but it was a moment of both heart and mind; for from that time there has been no looking back, only a deepening of commitment, a maturing of experience, a widening of horizons. All of these are grounded in that simple, biblical and evangelical experience of conversion and baptism within the fellowship of the Church. I was committed now. At home, at school, there was no doubt where I stood. And my timid and sensitive nature was strengthened and made bold by having to face a great deal of ragging and an incident or two of 'fisticuffs' because of the Gospel!

This experience also brought to the fore an ability to share and communicate which I had only feebly understood previously. From age twelve to sixteen I tentatively began to sing and pray publicly and even to take part in the devotional services and young people's work of the church. I was friendly, during this time, with groups of other Christians, some from the Pentecostal movement, and they spoke freely of an experience of the Holy Spirit which again sent me searching the pages of the New Testament.

God the Holy Spirit
By this time I realized that my early childhood experience was a valid experience of God, and I related it to God the Father quite explicitly. I was now very conscious of Jesus Christ as my Saviour, Friend and Brother. These were deeply held, experiential convictions which were shared within the church fellowship. The personal and the corporate were two sides of the same coin. But I realized that this was not enough; there was more, and I was restless and impatient to explore still further. At that time it seemed to me that the 'Holy Spirit' was the key to the situation, and as I read the Acts of the Apostles it did seem

21

that the local and organized church was lacking in this very dimension. I did have a somewhat narrow view of God's activity in the world at this time. I neglected my early intuitive understanding of nature as I became more influenced by a kind of fundamentalist Christianity which had a certain enthusiasm and dogmatic assurance, but was not always open to the freedom of God's action in other parts of the Church and the world.

However, at sixteen, longing for 'more of God', in a group prayer-meeting in an upper room I experienced an overwhelming experience of the Holy Spirit. It burned itself into the depths of my being, bringing with it an inebriation, freedom and emotional release which crowned my childhood and turned my shyness into boldness, courage and enthusiasm for God. It was an experience which was accompanied by the gift of tongues, and I found, some time ago, the old, tattered diary which says that I could hardly walk in a straight line to get home, and that the inebriation lasted six weeks, resulting in bringing five young people to commitment to Christ.

It was an enjoyment of God that ran over into ecstasy, and is aptly described by Michael Quoist as he refers to an experience that happened to me more than once, on cycle and motor-cycle:

> Words are inadequate to describe this loving embrace of God. The boy who is 'seized' by his Master right in the middle of the traffic, and has to dismount from his bicycle – suddenly unable to go on safely – will understand. . . . Also the boy who innocently confesses that he has to beg God to 'leave him for a while' at a gathering in order to be available to his friends.[2]

This third milestone in my spiritual pilgrimage has conditioned the rest of my Christian life up to the present time. There was no knowing, during that time, how or when this ecstasy would overtake me, and this is still so. alone on a cliff-top at Worm's Head Point on the Gower

Peninsula, entering into praise of God in tears and unutterable glory; in the gift of tongues after celebrating mass in a chalet at Butlin's Holiday Camp, Ayr, with a young people's group from St. Mary's Cathedral, Glasgow; on Christmas Day above Hilfield Friary on Batcombe Ridge in 1978, when I jumped and rolled down the turf singing in joy and wonder before the Lord . . .

A Trinitarian 'shape'

Basic to my spiritual pilgrimage has been an understanding of nature and grace in a trinitarian context. Let me explain. Classic trinitarian teaching says that each Person of the Holy Trinity participates in the life and action of the others; there is a holy inter-penetration of being and love. From this I understand that God (Father, Son and Holy Spirit) was at work in his fullness from my earliest days: so the Son and the Spirit were active in my early intuitive understanding of the divine, mysterious presence in the cosmos; the Father and the Spirit were at work in my evangelical conversion; and the Father and the Son were manifest in the experience of release which I identified with a baptism in the Holy Spirit.

All this has to do with the life of prayer, which for me has a trinitarian shape. I cannot operate with a Platonic conception of some 'philosophical Absolute', or some abstract 'Unmoved Mover' or 'First Cause'. My understanding of God is an experiential one, a biblical one, but a dynamic one. The Father loves the Son . . . loves the Spirit . . . loves the Father . . . And within the Body of Christ I am drawn into an experienced participation in the divine life of the Holy Trinity. The whole cosmos is caught up in such participation; the historic work of redemption and reconciliation which Christ effected is cosmic in its scope, and will be manifested throughout the whole created order.

A Hermit Symposium

It would not be fair to leave this chapter at this juncture, though I have made the point that the life of prayer is participation in the divine life of the Holy Trinity. It is necessary for me to indicate at least the direction my life has taken over the last decade. There have been a number of milestones that will become clear as we continue to share. But there was one particular week which more than any other concentrated both thought and feeling for me concerning the life of prayer.

Up to 1975 I had been a minister, a parish priest, and was on the staff of the Anglican Cathedral in Glasgow, and Anglican Chaplain to the University. I had a busy life of pastoral care, university involvement, and evangelistic engagements. My interior life was not keeping up with my busy schedule, and I realized, like many busy parish priests and workers, that I didn't have enough depth and experience to back up my preaching and teaching. Something had to be done. For some years I had been drawn to the 'religious life', but didn't envisage a contemplative community – I thought I was more of a friar than a monk!

I realized that to jump from such a loving congregation and fellow-clergy at St. Mary's Cathedral and from demanding but fruitful work at the Chaplaincy was not going to be easy. Also I was not at all sure which community I should try. I had lived for one academic year with a small but very wonderful hut community near Edinburgh, and this experience had stirred me up more deeply than I realized. Before me there seemed to be two options: either The Society of St. John the Evangelist at Oxford, or The Society of St. Francis.

But just then I heard of (and this sounds strange) a Hermit Symposium to be convened at St. David's, Wales, where hermit brothers and sisters from Orthodox, Roman and Anglican traditions were to spend a week of sharing and prayer together. It sounded a bit of a closed shop, but I managed to get myself invited, and lived for the week in the tranquillity of immense joy. I didn't re-alize all the implications of that week at the time, but I look back to it now and see that it was there and then that something happened within me that was both call and response, and to this day I am working it out.

Let me illustrate this week by three parts of a day. I remember one early morning eucharist, there were about thirty of us gathered in the Chapel behind the high altar of the Cathedral. It was a beautiful morning, and we were together to love and worship our Lord and to receive him in the sacrament of his body and blood. The morning sun streamed through the small, clear panes of glass in the window, and we lifted hearts and voices in worship in one of Charles Wesley's morning hymns:

> Christ Whose glory fills the skies,
> Christ, the true, the only Light,
> Sun of Righteousness, arise,
> Triumph o'er the shades of night;
> Dayspring from on high, be near;
> Daystar, in my heart appear.

After breakfast on that morning we had read one of the papers presented on early Celtic monasticism, and a silence fell upon the circle of gathered people. It was long, positive and restful. The sense of corporate sharing in the great tradition of prayer was powerful, and the veil between heaven and earth was thin.

Then one afternoon, I climbed along the rocks of the rugged and desolate Welsh coast and was exposed to the splendour and wildness of the waves breaking upon rocks and shore. Obeying the impulse of the moment I scrambled out of my clothes and jumped into the surfing waves, singing and shouting psalms and hymns in the context of the deep silence of that week. I recalled then that the Celtic monks used to stand up to their chins in the sea and sing or recite the psalms in enjoyment and praise of God!

These three experiences form a 'threefold cord' which could not quickly be broken, weaving together the strands of the evangelical nature of the Gospel, the deeper reaches of the life of prayer, and the cosmic revelation of divine mystery.[3] This memorable, formative week set my sights for the future; I continue to make my pilgrimage in its light.

I often reflect on that week, and wonder why it affected me so profoundly. The truth is that I was so aware that I was in the presence of men and women who were living out a vocation of prayer, that it bowled me over. It was not that they represented something beyond the grasp of ordinary Christians. Quite the opposite: by their very humanness, simplicity and humour, it was clear that they were truly human. They were nearer to what being human means than were the busy activists in church and world with whom I rubbed shoulders every day. I knew that God had created us to contemplate and reflect his glory – 'to glorify God and to enjoy him for ever', as the Westminster Shorter Catechism says. But here it was, a week in a dimension of prayer and love that impressed me by its simplicity and depth, beyond anything that can be expressed.

As I read more of the tradition and learned of the depth in prayer and solitude, several things became clear. I realized that scripture and psalms were the life-blood of such contemplative men and women, and necessarily so, for this way was difficult and thorny; it led through its own Gethsemane and Calvary, in identification with the Christ of God. I also knew that this was the way I would have to go, though of course the outward circumstances might be very different. I saw that within the religious life or not, just one thing was needful[4]: to enter into a contemplative love of God in Christ. Here I was, on the edge of entering into community life, hungering for the life of prayer with its roots deep into the mystery of the divine Love. And the Lord had brought me to a place where I could see, and feel, and know the reality, the power and the validity of a life dedicated to God in prayer.

Simple and total acceptance was called for. It was not a once-and-for-all decision, but a way which I could begin to take. The future was not clear, but to know the future was not necessary. I was to learn much more about darkness, loneliness, pain and solitude. Indeed, if I had known some of the things that lay ahead I would have hesitated – and that is still the case. But the Lord graciously reveals one step at a time, one day at a time, one moment in which to trust him.

My understanding of Calvary, for example, took on new dimensions. I had been well aware theologically and experientially of Jesus, the Lamb of God, entering into the depths of darkness and alienation on our behalf. The work of redemption was something which he alone could accomplish, and he *had* accomplished it fully through his life, atoning work and resurrection. I was full of wonder and awe at what he had done *for* me, *for* us; but I had not understood that what Christ accomplished *for* us, he desired to accomplish *in* us. We were to be identified with him in his Gethsemane, his Calvary, his Glory. I began to understand St Paul's Christ-mysticism in a completely new way, and his identification with Christ became a dynamic source of new light and power: '. . . that I may know him and the power of his resurrection, and may share his sufferings, becoming like him in his death . . .'⁵

The pain and glory of the Cross

The wonder and miracle of Calvary became double-edged for me. It was in Calvary that I experienced the strange mingling of joy and sorrow that were a part of our Lord's sufferings and glory, and which we are called to share. Part of my ongoing pilgrimage has been an ever-increasing familiarity with the loneliness and darkness of Calvary, and it is impossible for me to speak of the adventure of prayer and enjoyment of God without sounding the warning note of pain and darkness. A favourite mediaeval Franciscan, Jacapone da Todi, has a beautiful poem in his *Lauda* on the contemplation of the Cross, which is a dialogue between two friars, both of whom, if the truth be known, are part of Jacapone himself. And of me! One friar is filled with the joy, light and glory of the Cross, and the other feels its burning pain, loneliness and anguish:

First Brother

I was once blind, but now I see the light;
Gazing upon the Cross I found my sight.
Beneath the Cross my soul is glad and bright;
    Far from the Cross I am in misery.

Second Brother

Not so with me; this Light hath made me blind!
So fierce the lustre that around me shined,
My head is giddy, and confused my mind,
    Mine eyes are dazzled that I cannot see.

First Brother

Now can I speak, I that was once so dumb;
'Tis from the Cross that all my powers come;
Yea, by that Cross, of Thought and Love the Sum,
    Now I can preach to men full potently.

Second Brother

The Cross hath made me dumb, who spoke so well;
In such a deep abyss my heart doth dwell,
I cannot speak, and nothing can I tell;
    And none can understand nor talk with me.

These words exactly speak to my condition. 'Yea, by that Cross, of Thought and Love the Sum, Now I can preach to men full potently.' I have been preaching 'full potently' since my teen years, in churches, on street corners, on beaches, and while hitching lifts. But over the last years, my joy and gladness has been invaded intermittently and powerfully by personal and corporate sorrow and darkness, which is not incompatible with the glory, but interwoven with it. The last stanza above, even in translation, says it far better than I could – and the experience of glory and darkness lie together in my present experience.

I have known restlessness and perplexity in exploring my vocation to the relgious life, and at the same time have known dynamic joy in the Gospel, and peace in my heart. I have come to see that conflict and pain are part of deepening prayer and discipleship, and that one cannot separate the glory from the cross. For me the result has been an interior journey in which I find a profound response to words of William of S. Thierry:

> He with whom God is
>   is never less alone
> than when he is alone.
>
> For then he can enjoy his joy,
>   then he is his own
> to enjoy God in himself
> and himself in God.

The Trinitarian life of Prayer
In this chapter I have tried to describe a little of the threefold experience of my own pilgrimage in prayer: a childhood awareness of God the Father, a boyhood experience of conversion in Jesus, an adolescent initiation into the person and work of the Holy Spirit. All these are part of my retrospective understanding of creation and redemption. This chapter contains the seeds of the remainder of the book and reflects my personal path of prayer. It is rooted in human experience within the context of the Church's spiritual tradition. The journey is different for everyone, but the inexpressible joy and the participation of Calvary-suffering will reveal its own pattern to all who respond to God's loving embrace. There is infinitely more joy on ahead, and though I am afraid of the darkness, I must go on.

So I do not offer a systematic treatise on prayer, much less a scholastic treatment of the contemplative tradition. I feel I am beginning to wade into the river which proceeds from the throne of God,[6] after years of paddling on the edge. But before me there are waters up to my waist, waters to swim in, waters over my head, and the profound depths of the life of union and glory of God.

The two poles of joy and pain will continue in the work of sanctification, but I conclude this chapter with the words of Michel Quoist under his heading of '*Lord, You Have Seized Me*', and which appropriately describe where I am just now:

At times, O Lord, you steal over me irresistibly, as the ocean slowly covers the shore,
Or suddenly you seize me as the lover clasps his beloved in his arms.
And I am helpless, a prisoner, and I have to stand still.
Captivated, I hold my breath, the world fades away, you suspend time . . .
Thank you, Lord thank you!
Why me, why did you choose me?
Joy, joy, tears of joy.[7]

References

1 John 14:8, 9
2 Michel Quoist, *Prayers of Life*, pp. 110f. (Gill & Macmillan)
3 Eccles. 4:12
4 Luke 10:42
5 Phil. 3:10
6 Ezekiel 47:1-12
7 Quoist, *Op. cit.* p. 111.

2: Prayer:
Solitude and Darkness

Geographical Solitude

I sat cross-legged in the sunny doorway of the small wooden hut during six months' solitude in Dorset. It was midday and I had just said the office of midday prayer. Before me was the small vegetable garden, and all around was the wooded area of enclosure. Suddenly a golden brown fox emerged from the ferns and nettles to my right, and came up to within four yards of the hut. It had a long, slim body, a glorious full brush tail, sharp prick ears, and was very beautiful. At that moment a slight breeze blew over a page of my office book, and the fox looked up at me with piercing green eyes. It halted, paused, and quietly turned and crept back into the undergrowth.

That was a lovely moment in the geographical solitude in which I lived during the spring and summer of 1982, visited only by the animal creation – many birds, cows and sheep in the neighbouring fields, a pair of friendly pheasants, and our friary donkey, Jacomena, who would wander over for chapatis every day or so.

I have spent two such six-month periods of solitude; the first as indicated above, and the second during the autumn and winter of 1983/4 on the tip of the Lleyn Peninsula in North Wales, facing the holy island of Bardsey. The first experience was full of light with a patch of darkness in the midst of it. The second period included a lot of darkness, both spiritual and psychological, though glory was not absent. It is not right or appropriate for me to write of the inwardness of these experiences yet. They have not come to fruition, and there is another dimension which I have to explore before I can share more fully concerning them – if ever I can. But there were experiences and incidents during those two periods which will illustrate aspects of the deeper life of prayer, and they can be shared in this present pilgrimage.

Solitude of the Heart

It is not, of course, necessary to go off into geographical solitude to learn to live more deeply in prayer, in Scripture and in God. In fact, unless you can find God in the secret place of the heart in the midst of everyday noise and busyness, then physical solitude will be threatening and negative. I am not therefore advocating that you pack your bags and go off into the wild places which are left to us in these islands (though they are still to be found!). Rather, I am sharing some of my experience so that it will shed its own light on lives which have to be lived in the midst of family, work, and the unceasing demands upon time and energy.

I was, by this time, returning more and more to my early childhood experience of solitude, and had spent days and weeks in solitude from time to time. But busy parish and university life as priest and chaplain were draining time and energy, and although it seemed to the outsider that everything was well, that people were being drawn to the love of Christ and Christians were experiencing a deepening of their spiritual lives in church and chaplaincy, yet I was very aware of an inward need. It was not that I had not known periods of intense and gentle loving fellowship with God. It was not that I did not rest in Him as my Beloved. But my busyness and frenetic ministry was driving His gentle presence away. The Holy Spirit can be grieved and quenched not only by our sins and negligence, but also by our busyness and lack of loving attention.[1] I was not caught up entirely, but continually being drawn into the appealing network of a busy life, with a full diary and plans and projects to keep me and the Christians under my pastoral care busy for many a long day.

The Christian Church is filled with clergy and members who live under such compulsions – and it is exceedingly sad to find a pastor, a priest, a friar, a nun, who has become a 'workaholic', pacing up and down if there is nothing immediately on hand to fill up the next hour. Such a busy, organized, bureaucratic ministry is unable to lead people into the deep silence and solitude of the heart where God secretly dwells. One can live one's whole life in church and even in monastic structures without truly entering into an awareness of the divine presence, only to realize that awful fact at the moment of death.

Having been exposed to the powerful and yet gentle solitude of the brothers and sisters at the Hermit Symposium mentioned in the previous chapter, there was no longer any excuse for me. I had to listen to what had now become the voice of God, leading me into personal and spiritual solitude, and then for a time into physical and geographical solitude. For many a priest or parish worker, it would be at this point that God might draw them into the solitude of a retreat for a week or so in order to draw up a new plan of life and discipline. The demand of the Holy Spirit would be for a man or woman concerned to become less frenetic, to drop some of the 'good works', relationships, committees, meetings, projects, societies and religious observances in order to be alone with God. It would mean an inner transformation and an outward reformation of lifestyle, so that prayer would become the very life-breath of the believer, and not only a device for sustaining ecclesiastical work! Relationship with God must be transformed into that between lover and Beloved.

The way this is accomplished is different for everyone, but for me it was to become a friar. I was to begin a new pilgrimage, the shape of which was not at all clear, and the difficulties of which I could already envisage. After a false start, I found myself sharing for a time the life of one of our Anglican contemplative women's Orders in two of their houses. The first four months in the first house was sheer bliss. As well as some chaplaincy work and gardening, there was the daily and nightly round of monastic offices (liturgical prayers). The silence provided

33

an excellent context for prayer and study, and participation in a disciplined dedication to God was a positive strength at that time – not without the humour which is the hall-mark of genuine contemplative sisters!

The second four months in the second convent of the same Order I found frankly daunting! Here was the same dedication, the same round of day and night offices, but for me a lot of heavy digging and gardening, with no chaplaincy work and all my 'professional' expertise not needed, (they had an able chaplain). I suddenly became redundant, good-for-nothing in many senses, and I ceased to be appreciated, praised, adulated and needed. There was no waste of time or energy on flippant, bourgeois niceties, and all this was very good for me; it accomplished what years of 'ordinary' life had not been able to do.

Into the depths
I do not now want to give the impression that I lived in unrelieved gloom. There were precious moments of worship and love and humour mixed in with the life of silence and solitude. But I underwent a twofold purgation there. The first was a psychical/spiritual experience in which I felt the depths of my own loneliness and bankruptcy before God. The enclosure was radical, and one day as I was digging alone, I could see over the wall to where some men were labouring on a building site, with a cement mixer, a wheelbarrow, three or four labourers and one or two skilled craftsmen. The sounds of laughter and joking, of simple human sharing in work and friendship underlined my own emptiness. I found myself in such enclosure, surrounded by the convent walls, repeating the words which George Bernard Shaw puts into the mouth of St Joan when she was told that she was to be imprisoned for life:

> . . . to shut me from the light of the sky and the sight of the fields and flowers; to chain my feet so that I can never again ride with the soldiers nor climb the hills;

to make me breathe foul damp darkness, and keep from me everything that brings me back to the love of God . . . all this is worse than the furnace in the Bible that was heated seven times.

Running concurrently with this experience and contributing to it was another element. It was what I eventually realized was conflict with dark powers. A few days after arriving, I had felt a chilling blanket of heaviness descend upon me. I am not a depressive – quite the contrary, and what was happening to me was inexplicable and totally unexpected. This was to be the second period of an ongoing, positive experience which was to lead me to the place where I should enter more deeply into the life of prayer which had haunted me since the symposium at St. David's.

Instead of that I was being drawn into, even sucked under, by some strange heaviness that drained me of life and energy, that dulled my appreciation of earth, sea and sky, and that cut the nerve of my life of prayer and worship. This continued for a few days without meaning or rational explanation. There were no novelties to take my attention from the matter in hand, and of course, this was the intention of my spiritual director who had encouraged me to undertake this stay in this place. Outwardly I was my patient, cheerful self, and carried out the manual and liturgical work of the convent. But inwardly there was darkness and turmoil and a certain helplessness. Then about four days or so after the onset of this darkness, sitting in my stall in the chapel, I suddenly heard words which the Mother of the community had repeated to me nine months previously about the place. It concerned its geographical location and the possibility of areas of spiritual darkness which some people were very sensitive to. Our conversation had been brief, and she gave very little away on that occasion, and indeed my conscious mind had forgotten it. But now it was the clue, the key to the present situation. I knew its name, and knowing the name is the beginning of exorcism.

From that time on, I realized that I was set in that place as our Lord was set in the wilderness. I had been led (as Matthew and Luke say) and driven (as Mark says)[2] by the Holy Spirit into the wilderness for testing and temptation, to be exposed before God in my nakedness and to become aware of the activity of dark, spiritual powers. Many things I learned during this period of four months, but two of the primary lessons were: (1) that I had no business to lay claim to a vocation which was not mine, for if I did I should lay myself open to psychic damage; and (2) that even if there was the real possibility of vocation in solitude and the deeper life of prayer, the dimension of conflict with dark powers was an integral part of it, and could not be faced alone.

An examination of Scripture and of the experiences of the desert fathers had told me that previously – but here was experiential evidence which scared and challenged me. Before there was a risen life to live, there was a Calvary death to die. And I was tasting, just tasting, some of the pain and darkness involved.

Scripture has always been devastatingly challenging, judging and inspiring in my Christian experience, but it became life-blood to me now, as reflecting the heights and depths of God's dealings with men and women. It became the field in which the treasure was hidden, where I was to dig deeply for guidance, for inspiration, for clarification, and for which I would sell all that I had, like the man in the parable, to obtain the secret treasure.[3]

Two other pieces of writing came to my aid at that time to enable me to see clearly what was happening. They were both by Thomas Merton. One was his essay *The Cell*[4] in which he quite clearly lays down to those who have ears to hear, what it means to understand and obey the voice of God leading to the deeper life of prayer and discipleship. The second was almost his last book, entitled *Contemplative Prayer*, much of which is given over to a description of the stripping process of purgation and sanctification for that deeper union with God which is his will for all people.

I shall later refer to the threefold path of Purgation, Illumination and Union which is the classic unfolding of the mystical life of prayer, but the point I have reached in describing the second convent experience indicated that the first two stages had reversed their order. The Hermit Symposium at St. David's had been a period of illumination – full of joy and glory, heavy with promise. The first few months of my time with the contemplative community had been in continuity with that. But the second period had given way to a renewed purgation. I was challenged, scared, and faced with spiritual realities which were not to be trifled with.

I have written nothing as yet of the third state or degree, that of union. So great a mystical doctor as St. John of the Cross was reticent about direct speech concerning so ineffable an experience, and I have but glimpsed such glory; but its anticipation and promise was the interior work of the Holy Spirit who was my guiding light and hope even at this time.

Soon after this, I found myself back in the Society of St. Francis, involved in an exceedingly busy ministry of evangelism and pastoral care, while what I had learned burned itself into my mind and heart. I cannot indicate the debt I owe to my spiritual director during all this time. She dealt with me in patience and understanding, and allowed me to live through these experiences with just the necessary words of caution, advice, encouragement – and no more! She encouraged me in asking the Society to free me for the first, and then the second, period of solitude. Here again there was the exchange of the first two stages of the threefold way. It becomes necessary, at this point, to share something of these two periods.

References

1 Ephes. 4:30; I Thess. 5:19
2 Matt. 4:1; Luke 4:1; Mark 1:12
3 Matt. 13:4
4 Thomas Merton, *Contemplation in a World of Action*, 'The Cell'. (Allen & Unwin)

3: Prayer: Alone with God

A Personal and Shared Vocation

I have said that though we are all called to deepen our life of prayer and solitude of the heart, every one of us has a personal and particular path to tread. Our shared experience sheds its own light on one another's paths, and this is the purpose of my sharing. I am not 'allowed' by an interior sense of reserve, to share the centre of my time of solitude. Indeed, I am not *able* to share it, for it is in the realm of the inexpressible, which I cannot put into satisfactory thought-forms and concepts even for myself. I do not mean by that, that I entered into any profound mystical experiences, or that I levitated or bi-located or accomplished any of the feats that the monastic tradition says are of little use anyway (and often snares!). The fact is that there was a lot of emptiness, listlessness and boredom, to which I shall call attention later. But there were areas of height and depth which it is not appropriate to speak or write about.

However, there are many things I have communicated by spoken and written word which are appropriate to the present work, and the incomplete nature of this experiment in solitude does not mean that I cannot share some of the lessons learned so far. I think the best way to do this is to reproduce three cyclostyled letters I wrote in response to questions raised by friends who have followed me in love and prayer throughout this time and who continue to support and encourage me.

During the whole time of my noviciate in the Society of St. Francis, I had taken full part in all the elements that go to make up the life of a friar. I worked in the garden, painted and decorated, scrubbed and polished, cleaned out toilets, nursed the sick, did bookbinding and made sandals. I also preached the word, celebrated the sacraments, and did my share of evangelistic and ministry missions and conducted retreats on prayer and the spiritual life. But beneath the surface of all my activity was the growing longing for time and space to develop what had become a plant which I believed had been rooted by the Lord.[1] So talking with my spiritual director and the Guardian of the Dorset friary, I asked our Provincial Minister for permission to lay aside all engagements and commitments in the near future for a period of six months during which time I would go 'into the wilderness' of solitude to be alone with God.

The Society of St. Francis is what is generally known as a 'mixed' Order. It seeks to bring work and prayer together in a contemplative/active manner. Serious attention and priority is given to Scripture, prayer and worship, private as well as corporate. But place is also found for study, manual work, and self-sufficiency in vegetables, maintenance of buildings, cleaning, laundry, cooking. As well as all that, we look after guests and people 'in care', and do a great amount of social, educational, chaplaincy, evangelistic and pastoral work. We are, in short, a very busy community, with much prayer to undergird and sustain the active work. We have one brother who maintains a more contemplative lifestyle and a number of brothers who are feeling towards a more contemplative way. But my request was met with careful interest and something of a challenge to produce a theological explication of the meaning of such a period of solitude. This demand was very good for me, for it was needful to correlate the inward and intuitive yearning for prayer and solitude with a firm biblical and theological foundation. And that's just what I did!

I made it clear that I was but responding to something which had been initiated within me, and that this response was continually being tested by the tradition of contemplative and monastic prayer found in Scripture and in the desert fathers. I was not seeking a Platonic 'flight of the alone to the Alone', but a more profound understanding and union with God in Christ, by the power of the Holy Spirit. It was not solitude for solitude's sake, but was a response to God's call into the wilderness. And it was *for* and *with* the Society anyway. I was not intending to set up on my own. Not all members of the Body of Christ serve the same function. If the mouth is for speaking and the eye for seeing, there are some interior and hidden members and organs of the body whose work is vital and indispensible to the whole, and yet they are not seen, not heard, and not even felt.

The matter of place was not important to me at that point. I said that if certain safeguards were maintained it could be on friary land as long as it was out of earshot and visibility of the friary with its guests, coachloads, and curious tourists.

My profession as a friar contained my commitment to God and to the Society, and I made the point that I considered this a 'life-line' in spiritual, psychical and physical ways. Hermits have blind spots, and the challenge and its response calls for a certain strength of character which could at times become stubbornness of spirit, and a small group of sympathetic people are essential to support such a person in solitude.

The Provincial Minister and I explored the whole matter by correspondence and conversation, outlining the theological justification and the practical consequences of such a period. The outcome was that I received permission to withdraw for six months from March to September 1982, to live a life of prayer in an unspecified spot in a hut or caravan.

Preparation for Solitude
So in the midst of a busy friary life, the Guardian and I began scouting around for a site and a hut. It is an exciting story, for in our searching we shared much with one another. He had himself spent some months on a similar venture abroad, and felt and shared my quest with discernment and understanding.

One lovely evening about that time I went walking alone in a thickly wooded area over the hill from the friary and had a tremendous sense of presence and rightness about the place. It was as if the Lord had said: 'Well Ramon, here it is.' I got back and asked the friary gardening brother who owned the land. 'We do', was the reply, and I had a warm, tingling feeling of excitement. So we purchased a wooden hut, 12' × 6' (perhaps a bit too small), erected, lined and creosoted it. Jock, one of our guests, with his black labrador dog, lent his expert hands and eyes, and we fitted a bed, shelves, a camping gaz burner with two rings and a grill, and a water butt to catch roof rain, with a precarious lean-to and an Elsan loo behind.

The First Period
At the beginning of March I wrote to my supporting and praying friends, and here is the substance of the letter:

This letter comes to you with the desire to share concerning the next few months, and to ask your prayers. For a long time I have felt drawn into a period of solitary prayer, much in the biblical tradition and pattern of 'wilderness', and our Provincial Minister has given me permission to spend six months from 17th March to 17th September in such prayerful enclosure.

This means, among other things, that I shall not be writing on receiving letters – hence this present epistle to some close friends. It is not easy to write concerning the 'inwardness' of such a desire, or the meaning of such a period, but there are one or two things I want to share.

The first is that I understand this period as an affirmation of the primacy of God's love. I follow in obedience to what I feel is an inward call. Although it will be a time of solitary prayer in the sense that I shall be physically alone, it is certainly not isolation. My first desire in life is a closer union with God – Father, Son and Holy Spirit.

Wilderness is where men and women have experienced more deeply the communion of saints, and the powers of darkness! I am a professed brother of the Society of Saint Francis and am very much a part of the community in this venture, and I feel myself to be at the heart of the Church and a member of our common humanity. All these things are precious to me, and they are all clearly affirmed as I enter into solitude.

Prayer is the primary thing, saturated with scripture. There will be times of study, writing, manual work, etc., but the important thing will be that I am just 'there', open to God, and since I believe that it is He who has drawn me there, then the initiative must be with him as to the reason for my being there. I have a very firm framework of liturgical prayer, study, manual work, and a big patch of garden for vegetables – but any or all of this can be laid aside for the sake of silence and prayer.

I shall be remembering you especially at the eucharist and during the whole of Sunday morning prayer, so perhaps you will remember me especially as you go to worship on the Lord's Day.

I shall be 'sent off' from the friary at the Sunday eucharist and with a blessing early the next morning, when the Guardian will accompany me to the hermitage hut and we shall celebrate the first eucharist there. It is in the vicinity of the friary, but out of sight and earshot. There are always times of certain darkness and conflict in such a life, but I go trusting in the grace and sustaining power of our Father, resting in the love of our Lord Jesus, and indwelt by the Holy Spirit.

I feel strongly that the call to solitary prayer is part of the corporate life of the Body of Christ, and that in Him, I am united with all.

Throughout this book I shall be drawing on the experi-erience of solitude to illustrate the ways and pilgrimage of prayer. I continue to regard this experience as the kind of privilege that needs to be communicated in its overflow to others who are seeking to deepen their own lives of prayer in the midst of family, working and professional lives which are exceedingly busy. There is no need to enter into a detailed description of the period at this point, but I would say that I emerged reluctantly at the end of the six months, and was so overtaken by the personal questions and enquiring letters I received that I felt I had to make a real response. Apart from personal and group sharing which I did a great deal of during the following months, I sent out two 'pieces' of writing. One was an extended piece of poetry which I had written during the six-month period, the second was a letter answering practical and other questions which had been raised.

The poem was entitled 'Reflections on Solitude', and it is included in the appendix. It would be well to refer to it at this point. I had written it for my own purposes and not for distribution, but it seemed right to share it. It is in three parts as follows:

a. The first section enumerates the objections to such a wilderness period, calling into question its validity and veracity, and probing the motivation of such withdrawal.
b. The second section is a point-by-point evaluation and answer of the criticisms put forward in the first section, meeting them on their own ground.
c. Finally, there is a statement of the 'reasons of the heart', the core of the matter, the divine initiative which compels response.

This piece of poetry was accompanied by the more pragmatic kind of letter which set down the daily time-table, listed my concerns, manual work, study, and variations of mood. It also contained a summary of the possible consequences of such a solitary experiment, and this particularly elicited a great deal of comment and discussion. I reproduce the letter here:

October, 1982. I have been quite overwhelmed by the serious and enthusiastic interest that people have shown concerning my six months of solitude, and the implications for their own lives. It has been quite an experience to find how many people continually carried me in their prayers during the enclosure, and how important prayer is to so many, together with the desire for a deepening of the conscious awareness of the presence and experience of God. This letter is an attempt at response to the many questions which have been asked me both personally and by letter. There are so many that I cannot possibly write personally to answer those who have indicated their concern and sought guidance.

I enclose 'Reflections on Solitude' which deals with some aspects of my experience, and I hope this letter will fill in some other questions. As far as the practical and physical framework of the period is concerned, my day lasted from 4.00/4.30 am to 8.30 pm, and was divided approximately like this:

4.30 am	Night Office
5.15/5.30 am	Jogging (from 30–50 minutes)
6.30 am	Ablutions and breakfast
8.00 am	Morning Prayer and meditation
9.00 am	Study and prayer
12.00 md	Midday Office (eucharist on holy days)
1.00 pm	Main meal
2.00 pm	Manual work (vegetable garden, bookbinding, painting etc)
5.00 pm	Evening Prayer and meditation
6.00 pm	Light supper, followed by reading/study/ writing/prayer
8.30 pm	Compline and bed

There was quite a variation on some days. During the very hot weather I transferred manual work to the early morning, and when I felt the need for more prayer and 'passivity', I would put aside other work. I did not have

fast days at first, but then began to fast from sunset on
Thursday to sunset on Friday. Sundays were
different because after morning eucharist I spent the
morning in intercessory prayer, going through the
500 people on my list! The afternoon was my
recreation time, listening to the radio, making music
on my recorder, and producing two small pieces of
canvas work – which made Sundays differ from the
rest of the week.

When it comes to saying something about the
spiritual and psychical side of the life, it is difficult to
know what to say and how to say it. If you know me,
you realize that I am not often at a loss for words,
but this experience was one which I have long looked
forward to, and which encapsulated my deepest
longings and desires for God in love and prayer, and
I hardly know what to say about it. There were times
of intense longing and joy, times of darkness, conflict
and ambiguity, and shades of accidie between. But it
was all necessary, an experiment which has pointed
me in a certain direction more clearly, confirming
my feelings about contemplative prayer and my
involvement in such a life and vocation, although the
details have not been spelt out.

There were times when I was carried through
gospel scenes, participating in the life of Jesus, times
of study which brought me into a deeper awareness
of the presence of God in Scripture. And there were
times when I was drawn into the beginnings of a
more contemplative way which my heart longs for,
and for which this period of solitude has prepared
me.

I completed monthly reports for my spiritual
director, and copies went to our Provincial Minister
and the friary Guardian. These reflected the various
moods, joys, perplexities and awarenesses of the life,
as well as indicating my reading, study and physical
welfare. I sometimes found it difficult to write such
reports, and have left the retrospective evaluatory

report until the end of this year or beginning of 1983.

I have written elsewhere these words: 'I see the vocation of the solitary and hermit (or whatever you call one who is drawn to prayer in solitude), not as a cabbage-growing lover of nature who finds human contact not amenable, but one who obeys the inward prompting of the divine Spirit to prayer and intercession; one united in Christ's passion and sufferings, sharing already in the glory and victory of the resurrection, and girded with the armour of God in conflict with the powers of darkness for the redemption of the world and the manifestation of Christ in glory. 'All I care for', said St. Paul, 'is to know Christ, to experience the power of his resurrection, and to share his sufferings, in growing conformity with his death . . . It is not to be thought that I have already achieved this. I have not yet reached perfection, but I press on, hoping to take hold of that for which Christ once took hold of me . . .'. (Phil. 3:10–12). This is what it is all about!

I am grateful to the Society of Saint Francis for the permission and opportunity to have experienced such a period of solitude, as a member of the community. I had three 'official' visits from the Provincial Minister and Guardian, and the remarkable thing is that no-one discovered where I was, and I was left completely alone in an overgrown wooded solitude in which there was freedom for me to live and respond to the Holy Spirit. I knew that whatever happened, I would stay there – even if I found it very difficult. The fact is that it was sheer joy – and even the dark days were good and necessary in the context of the whole period.

It was, as I have said, an experiment, and I previously outlined the possible result of such a time in the following way:

1 It could lead to a deepening appreciation of solitude and to a solitary vocation;

2 It could lead to a contemplative life with others in a kind of lavra or skete;

3 It could lead to a principle of biblical alternation –
   three or six monthly periods in silence, and
   the rest of the year in some apostolic and SSF
   work;

4 It could lead to an abandonment of solitude,
   returning to active life in the Order as the
   primary thing;

5 It could lead to psychological disturbance.

I'm glad to say that number 5 did not become
operative! It was St. Patrick's Day when I left the
community chapel with Brother Bernard, and we went
with incense and prayers to the wooded enclosed area.
We marched around the whole area, censing, singing
and praying, and when we got to the hut we prayed
around it and within it, celebrating mass and
sanctifying it all, including the potential vegetable plots
to the Lord. I emerged six months later for the mass
of the Stigmata of St. Francis – how strange it was to
be physically with people again – I became hoarse at
the end of the first day!

I realize that in writing this letter I have 'skirted
around' the interior effects and consequences of the
experience. Part of the reason is that I cannot really
speak about it, and part because I don't know
altogether what has happened in my own life. It may
be appropriate to quote some words I wrote in a letter
after a few days in our hermitage in February 1980:
'Yesterday I went walking into the Batcombe woods;
the trees were stark and bare, the brown leafy mould
was soft beneath my feet, and I felt the sadness and
glory of human love, and how it reflects and reaches
for that which it symbolises in the source and fullness
of the divine Love. So much of my understanding of
love is reflected in the cosmos, and the February
solitude captured the way in which my own pilgrimage
manifests the sad absence of my Lord. And yet,
though the sun filtered weakly through the trees, and
the soft wind was cold, the whole atmosphere held
promise, and I could feel the soft breathing of the

life beneath my feet. All this is within my own heart – and in the solitude I *feel* the response which I merely *believe* when surrounded by the busyness down below in the friary. No, that's not entirely true, for so often I am invaded by joy or pain, and the Lord touches my heart in communication with others. But solitude is the context of my inward search – and I *must* continue for I cannot live without that Love which I have only glimpsed, but glimpsing causes me to long for it . . .'

That is enough for now, those who need to know more will learn it from me or elsewhere in the Lord's good time. Pray for me – in what an adventure of GLORY we are involved – in spite of all opposition!

One of the nice incidents about the summary list of consequences above was that Brother Anselm, seeing this before I began, took hold of the fifth point – that such an extended period could lead to psychological disturbance:

Brother A: 'What do you mean by psychological disturbance?'
Brother R: 'Well, that a person exposed to himself in solitude could slip over the edge. He could go dotty.'
Brother A: 'Yes! Will that not happen to you?'
Brother R: 'No, I don't think so.' (with a wide grin)
Brother A: 'And why not?'
Brother R: 'Well I'm a bit dotty already – isn't it a bit daft going off alone for six months with nobody and nothing? But also I have a good sense of humour and know I'm a fool and can laugh at myself.'

Brother Anselm responded in his own inimitable way – and has encouraged me all along the way ever since.

Although, as I said in the above letter, I was not able to

communicate the 'centre' of prayer in solitude, it was clear to me that God was at work interiorly confirming His word and communicating His loving presence. All I had to do was to respond in both discipline and spontaneity. It was clear that I was being carried through the whole gamut of human emotions, from ecstasy through boredom to darkness and fear.

As soon as I returned to life in community, there was a list of engagements to fulfil, and wherever I went, people young and old wanted to know about the experience of solitude, the meaning of prayer beyond the borders of their own experience. And I got involved in sharing in word and experiment with groups who came to the friary, and with groups of committed people in local and mission parishes.

One would not immediately correlate the hermit tradition with direct evangelism, but it was the case that when I met non-Christians in groups or in my hitch-hiking experiences around the country, they asked questions about the life of a Franciscan friar. They almost always warmed to the subject and were anxious to know more, not only about the alternative life-style of such Christian 'communism', but also about prayer in solitude.

It was a great joy, between that first period and the second period of solitude in 1983/84, to share methods and techniques of silence, meditation and prayer with groups of all ages and denominations. And since that experience I have found myself ministering not to so many people in such an explicitly evangelistic manner, but to fewer people in greater depth. This is certainly one of the direct consequences of prayer in solitude.

The Second Period

When I returned from that first six months, although I tried to enter into the work of communication and ministry with my old enthusiasm, I found that my heart was still in the wilderness with God. Of course, it was not that the Lord was not with me in the ministry, in my brothers and sisters, and in the people to whom I ministered. Certainly, unless the Lord is known and indwelling his temple interiorly, then solitude or marketplace are equally vain. Nevertheless, it became clearer that my whole perspective had changed, and that I was living from the depths of the silence and prayer that I had learned in the six months. The analogy I found myself using was that I had previously launched out from the harbour of the community, and was carried along by the current of evangelism, while there was a deeper but quieter undercurrent of prayer. What was now happening was that the deeper and stronger current of prayer and solitude was carrying me, so that the current of evangelism was no longer primary.

There is a sense, of course, in which every Christian is a person of prayer and an evangelist. The very fact of the indwelling Christ means communion with God and communication of the loving and reconciling Gospel – which is evangelism. But there is such a thing as a primary ministry and vocation. Not everyone is called to stand on a street corner or in a pulpit to proclaim and expound God's word, and not everyone is called to the ministry of full-time intercession, or has a gift of healing or prophecy. It all depends on God's particular call, 'apportioning to each one individually as he wills.'[2] But now I was finding a change in perspective, in direction, and a profound response in my heart to the call of God into the wilderness: 'I will lure them away, lead them into the desert and speak to their hearts.'[3]

At this time I led a mission to the Anglican and United Reformed Churches in Bracknell, Berks., and another at Ketton, Lincs. I was the Franciscan missioner at Keble College, Oxford, during the 1983 Oxford Mission, conducted retreats at the Othona Community in Dorset, led numbers of groups in study and prayer, and shared in the continuous ministry from the friary. Then there was the month-long mission up and down the geographically long diocese of Swansea and Brecon. In all these activities there was joy and response and hard work, and they were all undergirded by prayer all round. But all the while I was living at another level where the solitude of God was drawing me to itself.

Something had been clearly initiated in the first period that was not complete, and a second such period was indicated. There was a dimension which had not been granted, and I could see no further forward than another such period. What I did not know, though I had been warned, and my spiritual director was well aware of it, was that a second such period would bring with it a dimension of darkness, conflict and pain. 'The honeymoon is over,' as one wise priest said to me, 'don't expect the glory that you found the first time.' They were right, of course. I had been warned, I had a certain imaginary expectation of it – but one can only realize it in the actual experience.

As the three of us put our heads and hearts together, (viz. my spiritual director and the two friars who were over me in the Lord), it became clear that (a) there should be a second period of solicitude; and (b) that it should be geographically distanced from the friary.

From the time that Bardsey Island and the Lleyn Peninsula was mentioned, it became clear that this was the area. I was averse to looking to Wales lest it should seem that I was cultivating some kind of romantic or sentimental attachment to the Celtic hermit tradition which I was so enamoured of anyway! Remember, it was the Hermit Symposium at St. David's that was the primary moving factor in all this!

But our Provincial Minister brought me the address of a friend who was farming at the tip of the Peninsula, near Aberdaron, and had a small stone cottage which she rented out in the summer months. It was unoccupied during the winter because of the bleak, though beautiful outlook and the tremendous gales from the Irish Sea.

Soon it was fixed up. So fourteen months after I had emerged from the first period, I entered a second period. But this time it was during the Autumn and Winter months in a wild and beautiful party of the North Wales coast.

It is an over-simplification, but it does give a fair general picture to say that if the first period was full of light, gladness and assurance with a patch of darkness in the midst of it, the second period pitched me into a certain loneliness and darkness. This did not happen immediately, but the stark reality of Winter solitude soon came upon me.

My spiritual director had said that the season and terrain were part of the exercise. The Dorset period was light and gladness through Spring and Summer, and now the mountain terrain, the bleak, cold days and nights, the winds and sea, reflected heaviness, mystery and darkness. I included this paragraph in my covering letter in my first report to her:

. . . I do not know what the outcome will be – I already see that the golden sunshine and quiet beauty of a Dorset summer in green woodland is past, and the Winter among the cliffs and rocks of the Lleyn Peninsula with the heave and swell of the restless sea has caught me already in its mood. As I write, darkness and mist fall over the mountain, the cry of the high wind echoes around the cottage and the dim outlines of the surrounding rocky heights bear witness to the austerity of the months to come. But the mystic fire burns within, and the longing for the Beloved and the pain of absence mingle in the way that opens before me.

Also, the fact of the Island of Bardsey was a powerful and solitary witness to solitude. Sometimes it loomed dark and menacing out of the turbulent waters off the Peninsula. Sometimes it would catch and reflect the glorious sunset over a still and golden sea. But always, being the island of 20,000 saints, it had a quality of the numinous, of awe and mystery – and a spiritual quality which was threatening as well as glorious. I felt the Peninsula in its pagan as well as its Christian setting. The whole feel of the place changed not only with my changing moods, but I felt it sometimes imposed its own mood upon me. Contemporary writers on Christian spirituality speak of the island and the Peninsula with great awe and reverence,[4]; it is certainly one of the secluded holy places of the Christian tradition.

Prayer Support and Second Letter

Around the Dorset friary there are a number of parishes which the friars serve, preaching and celebrating the eucharist, where prayer and healing groups have sprung up over the last few years. From such loving and praying people I had immense support. Some weeks before I set off for the Lleyn Peninsula I devoted a sermon to answer some of their questions about the meaning and pattern of withdrawal into the wilderness for the sake of the divine Love. The body in prayer, physical well-being, and vegetarian diet came into the sermon and the talks afterwards. And so, from Yeovil to Dorchester, came gifts of food and letters of encouragement. On the labels of bottled beetroot and tinned beans were texts from Ezekiel, the Psalter, Isaiah and the Gospels, and requests for prayer for the old, the sick and the needy.

Some of the glory and darkness of that period will form part of the prayer instruction of these pages, but to this extended group of supporting people I felt I ought to write after the conclusion of the second period of solitude. I reproduce the letter below because it also communicates the feel and mood of that amazing place on the Lleyn Peninsula:

May 1984
You are among the friends who have prayed for me during the last six months of solitude and prayer on the Lleyn Peninsula, and for whom I have prayed, especially on the Sunday mornings, during my particular time of intercession. It is not possible for me to write personally (I found over 60 letters and cards on my return), but this letter will indicate in a small way how things have gone.

It becomes more difficult to speak about the content of my experience as I go deeper into the solitude and prayer. This is true to the ways of human love, how much more of the divine Love? But I have written some things, and I shall share a few paragraphs penned during the very wonderful period from November last year to earlier this month. The 'quote marks' indicate passages from my journal . . .

'I am here. The tiny stone cottage, 100 years old, is built into the Anelog mountain, just below the peak which faces the Island of Bardsey, ''Island of 20,000 saints''. The movement from the month's mission to solitude was sudden and dramatic, with one day intervening. . . .

'I am amazed at the way I have come – how could it be possible that I should find myself here alone, and how amazing that I am learning the goodness and severity of God in it all. I am not unaware of the severity, the darkness, the grief, the pain that I have stored within me. There are hours of days of silent weeping still; there is the aching love and loneliness and longing. But there is also, because of this, the awareness of the divine Love, the mystery of the dark night, and the path of purgation leading to illumination and union with God. I am becoming aware of the unity of the whole pattern, of the interweave of human love and grief, and of the fact that not one thread will be missing, and that the warp and woof of his weaving will bring me to death and to life. It is not a way I could have chosen, though I see that I have chosen it; it is not a way I could desire, though I do desire it more than all; it is not a way that I can take, for I am afraid – but I do take it with courage and strength and fear and glory.

'There is much that haunts and paralyzes me in my human weakness, but there is also the strength that fills me so that I can fly into the open vistas of eternity. Before me though is bleakness, both physical and spiritual. I believe that much of this time will be lived out in such darkness that is not possible for me when I am with others. In evangelistic and apostolic work people observe the energy, the glow, the enthusiasm which has been part of my Christian experience from a child. They cannot see my tears, my darkness, and the answering within me to the barren rocks and desolation of this mountainside. I hear the rising sighing of the wind around the mountain as darkness falls now, and the answering heave and swell of the sea, and my heart cries out in echoing loneliness on the path of love . . . and yet the hunger and thirst is infinite, and I cannot rest in human love alone. For this I have known all my emptiness, and only this way will I know, and come to the divine Love. Whether that will be in this life or beyond death I cannot tell, and it is not mine to be concerned – but I travel the way I must go, with the results I do not know, with no longer the concerns and fears I used to have . . .'

The preceding paragraphs from my journal reflect the deep longings and experiences of my heart in solitude. I have now returned to Dorset and am engaged in the life and ministry of the friary, retreats and parish work. But my heart is in the solitude of God – whether in Dorset or North Wales does not matter. It is not confined to a geographical location, though I must say that the Anelog and Bardsey Island area was both menacing and glorious in mystery and holiness.

Before I conclude this letter with more words from the last days of my journal, I want to say how grateful I am to those who not only prayed for me throughout the time (and this was the primary thing), but also gave me edible and other gifts so that there was no fear of me starving to death! The great kindness of the parishes around the friary, and friends of SSF was manifest in most concrete ways. I packed our vehicle with tins of coffee, dried milk, beans, spaghetti, rice, fruit, tomatoes, Christmas cake, preserved fruit, jams, marmalade, dried fruit, lentils, beans of all varieties (soya, mung, field, black-eye, haricot, butter and kidney!). My vegetarian diet was rich in protein of right combinations, and I remain as healthy as ever – an important factor in living alone.

So in the last days of the six months I wrote: '. . . I am preparing to leave this place with a certain sorrow and an immense sense of gratitude. The few people who know what the life of prayer in solitude is about forecast that the second period would not be the 'honeymoon' experience of light and glory as was much of the former Dorset period, but they assured me of their prayers and of the rightness of the way. I had confidence in their words and was partially prepared for the darkness and emptiness. But one can never live imaginatively an experience which has to be undergone existentially. There has been the realization that I cannot bear the challenge or demands of the deeper life of prayer that I had hoped to experience without complete dependence on God's grace. But there has also been the awareness that such a call or invitation is a sheer gift of grace, and that "he who has begun the good work will perform it . . ." As well as times of darkness and helplessness there have been periods of interior joy and a deeper understanding of my part in the mystery of salvation, as a man, as a friar, as part of the Body of Christ.'

I am not in a position yet to reflect adequately on the complementary nature of the two periods of solitude, and shall not do so until some months have passed. But I am well aware that both periods seem to me to be the result of my obedience within SSF to the call of God to an exposure to the Gospel in solitude. I do not emerge with any great resolution to my, or the world's, problems, though much of my prayer has been concerned with the threat of nuclear catastrophe. Neither have I a blueprint for future ministry and vocation. But I do affirm the integral nature of solitude in my own pilgrimage, and look forward to the unfolding of the immediate future. It looks as if I shall soon be transferring to our monastery in Worcester, and that also seems right, wherever the path may lead from there.

I am blessed with discerning spiritual direction from those who share with me in this adventure from within our own Society, and from the Sisters of the Love of God. Whatever the outcome, I cannot but be immensely glad of the opportunity of the last six months in such a place at such a time. It can only serve to deepen my life of prayer and ministry in the Church and the world.

One of the most precious experiences of the time was to descend into the depths beyond my own individuality into a profound corporate sense of our common humanity with its pains and joys, and to find that the divine Love is in and through all, and will ultimately be manifested as 'all in all'.

In the grace and love of our Lord Jesus Christ,

I have written this particular chapter in order to share two of the most intimate and wonderful experiences of my life, which illustrate for me a particular way in which Jesus' words may be understood: '. . . where your treasure is, there will your heart be also.'[5] Heaven is where the presence of God makes itself manifest – at the burning bush, on the mount called Sinai or Hermon, Tabor or Calvary – and there will be the treasure, and there one's heart. The wilderness can be a place of glory or a place of fearful emptiness and death; a place where the shekinah glory descends, or a place where the devils gather. It was both for our Lord, and it is for those who follow him.

But these two periods were also for me a place of trembling. They caused me to quake before the living God, at times with a sense of awe and wonder, as He revealed Himself in creation and redemption in the blinding glory of the world around and in the darkness and splendour of the cave of my own heart. It was a calling away from preaching, communicating, counselling, lecturing, into emptiness, bleakness, darkness and yet glory. Thomas Merton says that the true solitary is not called to an illusion, to the contemplation of himself as a solitary, but to the nakedness and hunger of a more primitive condition. That is of a stranger and wanderer on the earth, called out of the familiar in order to seek strangely and painfully after he knows not what.

I want to record that after this second period I realize that I have not yet learned what must be learned. It is being unfolded gradually. I have had to wait many years for it to begin, and it seems that I have experienced the positive fullness and glory of lesson one, and been plunged into the loneliess and darkness of lesson two (rather like the stages of purgation and illumination transposed that I spoke of earlier). I suppose lesson three has to do with the beginnings of union with God, the very thought of which causes a profound trembling in my body and spirit. Certainly my life has been turned upside down by these experiences, and though I would not deny my gregarious love of human beings, my joy in little children, and my ability and enthusiasm for communication, yet the power of the call of the desert draws me away into a solitude in which I am nearer to all humanity in the silence of God. Peter Anson's words were quoted in the Hermit Symposium:

> There are always likely to be some men and women who feel that 'material' solitude is essential for their spiritual life. They can no more do without it than without food or drink, and if they are deprived of this isolation their lives become spoilt, cramped and distorted, and they never find their true vocations. The 'born solitary' is drawn to an eremitical life for various reasons, partly natural, partly supernatural . . . They discover that they need to separate themselves from their fellow-creatures in order that their latent powers may have room for expansion and growth, that they be more fitted to serve mankind generally.[6]

The sharing of my experiences in these pages is in order that you may enter imaginatively and prayerfully into the place which you need to know and recognize as your own. If my communication of such basic human experience invites you to a desert scrutiny of your own life in the presence of God, then I shall have achieved my aim. As Mother Mary Clare SLG quoted in concluding her paper at the Hermit Symposium:

> The hermit is simply a pioneer . . . in the way of the desert which the whole of humanity must follow of necessity one day, each one according to his measure and his desire. This eremitical vocation, at least embryonically, is to be found in every Christian vocation, but in some it must be allowed to come to its full flowering in the wind of the Spirit. It is not enough to affirm that the thing is good in itself, it is necessary that the Church and society do something, so that this life may be realizable, so that each may at least touch it, be it only with the tip of his little finger.[7]

References

1 Psalm 1:3
2 1 Cor. 12:11
3 Hosea 2:16
4 See A. M. Allchin, *The World is a Wedding*, pp. 114–118. London: (Darton, Longman and Todd, 1978).
5 Luke 12:34
6 A. M. Allchin (ed), *Solitude and Communion*, *Papers on the Hermit Life* given at St. David's, Wales, by Orthodox, Roman and Anglican contributors, p. 70 Oxford: (Fairacres Publication, 1977).
7 *Ibid.*, p. 76.

Part II: Experiment

4: Prayer and the Body

The Relationship of Mind and Body in Prayer

The Body in Worship

Exciting things are happening in the Church as a result of catholic renewal, evangelical awakening and charismatic teaching. It is not now unusual to go to a liturgical eucharist where one of the great mass settings is being sung, together with colourful vestments, incense, a powerful biblical homily, and in the midst of all this, between the reading of epistle and gospel, a liturgical dance may be performed, celebrating the Scripture reading or the theme of the service.

'The body in worship' is in! It is possible liturgically and publicly to worship God with eyes, ears, hands, feet, smell and touch. The 'washing of feet' ceremony and regular 'laying on of hands' are becoming familiar sights in our pattern of worship. We may now use bread and wine, water and incense, wax and flame, charcoal and oil to glorify God in the body and in the spirit which are God's.[1]

In the Incarnation, God prepared a body for his Son,[2] and he has for every one, male and female. A heresy which has dogged the steps of the Western Church, Catholic and Protestant, is based in Greek dualism, an important philosophical understanding which has its roots in Gnosticism, Manichaeism and misinterpreted Platonism. The Western Fathers in particular were tainted by this dualism which held the body suspect. Augustine never really threw off some of the ideas of Mani, and in revolt against his former manner of life, viewed human reproduction and sexuality with grave suspicion.

Much of this is understandable, and is based in human experience. But in order to understand what the Bible says about the body, one has to experience both the positive and negative poles which is the Bible's response to the ambiguity we all feel. There are times when we feel the vibrant radiance and energetic potentiality of the body, conceived in the embrace of loving communion, and destined for immortality. And there are times when we experience the sin that has made it a body of death, heavy with lust, living in darkness, weighed down by sickness, and destined for a mouldering earth to be consumed by worms.[3]

Sometimes, when swimming in the ocean, running or pedalling along with the wind blowing through one's hair, refreshed after a shower, or waking to another glorious day of vitality and friendship, the body is a friend to be listened to, enjoyed and loved, 'for no man ever hates his own flesh, but nourishes and cherishes it . . .' says Paul.[4] At other times it is a stumbling block, suspect, ambiguous, and if in dominance can lead into the physical manipulation of others, and to interior emptiness.

A biblical theology faces this ambiguity, and gives the answers 'yes' and 'no' to the body's demands. It does not believe in nature apart from grace, but neither does it affirm grace without nature. The *imago Dei*, God's likeness in created man, has been distorted, deprived and twisted away from the truth, but the image is not totally destroyed. Grace regenerates, purifies, elevates and fulfils nature. It restores and builds upon nature, and at the last, salvation will embrace the whole created order, transfiguring it in resurrection glory.[5] Moses, Stephen, and pre-eminently Jesus, participated in the glory of physical transfiguration as a foretaste of resurrection.[6] We already receive the seal of the Spirit of God in anticipation of the day of the redemption of the body. We receive our forgiveness, reconciliation, and divine indwelling, being sealed with the promised Holy Spirit 'who is the guarantee of our inheritance until we acquire possession of it . . .'[7]

The Christian ideal is that the purified and enlightened spirit vitalises and guides the body, so that the whole person is dedicated to God in love and joy. 'So we do not lose heart. Though our outer nature is wasting away, our inner nature is being renewed day by day.'[8]

The biblical doctrine of salvation was never meant to indicate merely the rescue of the 'soul' from the consequence of sin. The scope is much wider than that and has to do with 'spirit, soul and body',[9] and Jesus is the Saviour of the body.[10] We should glorify God in our body not only by avoiding immorality, but by actually experiencing the fact that our bodies are temples of the Holy Spirit who dwells within us.[11] To present our bodies to God in holy dedication and physical offering is our spiritual worship.[12] The more one participates in the physical part of one's being in worship, the more the whole symbolism of the Church as the Body of Christ will become alive as part of our ongoing experience.[13]

The wide application of the word 'salvation' embracing body, mind and spirit is envisaged by Paul: 'May the God of peace himself sanctify you wholly; and may your spirit (*pneuma*) and soul (*psyche*) and body (*soma*) be kept sound and blameless at the coming of our Lord Jesus Christ.'[14] The apostle maintains that the Holy Spirit dwells within the regenerate spirit of man, revitalising even his mortal body. He uses the word *sarkos* for the corruptible and sinful fleshly nature which we may translate as 'sinful flesh', but *soma* for the flesh in which salvation is fulfilling its ministry of quickening and healing. So we find in Romans 8:8: '. . . they that are in the flesh (*sarkos*) cannot please God.' But in verse 11: 'But if the Spirit of him who raised Jesus from the dead dwells in you, he who raised Christ Jesus from the dead will give life to your mortal bodies (*soma*) also through his Spirit which dwells in you.' The same truth is emphasized in the great resurrection chapter in the letter to Corinth.[15] The indwelling Jesus is the principle of mortal and spiritual life in a powerful statement of the saving gospel in the second Corinthian letter:

But we have this treasure in earthen vessels, to show that the transcendent power belongs to God and not to us. We are afflicted in every way, but not crushed; perplexed, but not driven to despair; persecuted, but not forsaken; struck down, but not destroyed; always carrying in the body the death of Jesus, so that the life of Jesus may also be manifested in our bodies. For while we live we are always being given up to death for Jesus' sake, so that the life of Jesus may be manifested in our mortal flesh.[16]

The point we are making is that as the Old Testament does not think of man as disembodied spirit but understands the *shalom* of salvation to include the whole of man, so the New Testament envisages salvation as applicable and appropriate to the totality of man's being. The unfolding of salvation is in process according to New Testament perspective. We *were saved* at the cross when Jesus cried: 'It is finished'; we *are being saved* daily as we walk in the Spirit, and we *shall be saved* at the *parousia*, the appearing of our Saviour, 'who will change our lowly body to be like His glorious body, by the power which enables him even to subject all things to himself.'[17]

The Body at Prayer
If the body is to offer itself as part of our whole worship, it has its particular part to play in prayer and in appropriating the awareness of God's presence. Not only do we use our ears to hear the word of God and our vocal organs to praise him in word and song, we also use our lifted hands to bless his name, to clap his praise, and our feet and bodies to dance to his glory. The psalmist envisages lying down, sitting, rising up,[18] walking, standing, dancing; kneeling or prostrating oneself is also a posture of prayer.[19] Posture and bodily stance express an attitude to God as well as to man, and we shall see how important posture, breathing, heartbeat and pulse are in the life of prayer.

A Christian audio-visual review magazine contains

details of the Bible Society's book in the creative resources series, entitled *Move Yourselves*.[20] It is subtitled 'Exploring the Bible in movement, mime and dance'. The authors provide a programme for exercise, movement, and corporate communication of biblical truth in drama, mime and dance. Our bodies are not only functional units, they say, but are to be used in worship. Also reviewed in this magazine is the series *Workout with God*, which uses physical and athletic symbolism to convey the importance of disciplined Bible study, and a video package which I have not seen but find intriguing, is called *Aerobic Celebration*, and consists of intermediate and advanced aerobic exercise to what the publishers call 'Christian music'(!). I do not intend a section on aerobic and miming video reviews, but there is much more material on both the secular and Christian market to cause us to sit up and take notice. Our own brothers and sisters of the Society of St. Francis are exploring mime and movement as a means of evangelistic communication, and recently performed a gospel mime on the green before Sherborne Abbey. Our present purpose is to use the body in prayer.

Stillness and Silence

Let us first of all think about stillness of body and silence. It is easier to be frenetically active than to be still, easier to work up a sweat by jogging than to 'study to be quiet'.[21] But if one is to make any progress in prayer this is a primary consideration, and if one cannot wait upon God in silence and be still before him,[22] then it is simply true that no life of prayer will follow.

Inward stillness is the basic attitude, but this includes stillness of the body. The interplay between body and mind is so intimate that one stimulates the other. Our Lord Jesus carried an interior stillness with him wherever he went, and communicated his own quality of peace and rest[23] to those who were in bodily or spiritual need. Not only did he call his disciples apart to a desert place for refreshment and communion, but he frequently went into solitude himself on the lake, into the mountains, and often continued all night in prayer.[24] He went into the wilderness for a long period, drawn and driven by the Spirit.[25] What heights and depths of loving communion with the Father and the Spirit he knew, and what conflict with dark powers he endured we can only imagine. But if entering into solitude, silence and such mystery was part of his pilgrimage, how much more should it be ours.

Experiment with Relaxation and Posture

Sooner or later we shall have to stop reading and thinking about all this and put it into practice. Let's start with posture. We need a quiet place where we shall not be disturbed. 'Go into your room and shut the door,' says Jesus, 'and pray to your Father who is in secret.'[26] If you have no spare room, then use the garden, the garden shed, your local church or a secluded field. People who are in love always manage to find a place to be alone together, to be lost in each other's presence, and to enter into loving and intimate communion. So it is with the Lord.

Now as a prerequisite to your chosen posture, practise an exercise in relaxation. It is best to wear either singlet and shorts or a track suit – nothing tight-fitting and no footgear. Everything free, everything easy, no strain. Now lie down upon the ground on your back, and very simply enumerate the parts and areas of your body, from your feet . . . calves . . . thighs . . . buttocks . . . abdomen . . . arms . . . hands . . . shoulders . . . neck . . . to your face and head. As you enumerate, stretch and gently relax each part . . . letting go . . . letting go . . . until you have drained the tension away and you are at rest. Resting naturally, and resting in God.

I have found, after becoming familiar with this form of relaxation, that it is an appropriate way to meditate upon one's death. Did that sentence suddenly give you a jolt? Unless we have come to terms with our own finitude and mortality, we had not truly begun to live, let alone to pray. Certainly the life of prayer in Christ is a continual dying and rising, and Jesus tells us that to follow him is a going down into death.[27]

The seemingly strange thing about solitude and silence is that the more one is exposed to oneself and to the world of nature, the greater the awareness of natural rhythms, both of the body and of the natural world. Whatever benefits may accrue to technological man, the danger is that he may lose touch with his deep, inward self. Incessant external but superficial activity engages his cerebral functions but neglects the area of the intuitive – the heart. That is why, on the one hand contemporary man has lost a deep sense of God, of prayer and of the truly corporate, and on the other manifests a novel curiosity and thirst for a contemplative dimension. It is possible now to introduce a VIth form comprehensive school group to contemplate techniques of prayer and meditation and not be laughed out of court. It is no longer a novelty to be invited to a large comprehensive school on missions, to speak to one of the morning assemblies, and to do the rounds of various forms and groups with great interest and discussion of metaphysical and spiritual questions. I visited ten schools in the November 1983 mission and in the upper age ranges, in the wide context of 'reciprocative humour' I actually shared and communicated experiences of the life of prayer, and learned some basic computer techniques from the pupils!

The point we are making about relaxation in terms of posture is that there are some postures which predispose the body to meditation. If the body is the temple of the Holy Spirit, then the ideal is to be free from disease. In other words, to possess a sane mind in a healthy body, with a freedom from tension which comes from an inward tranquillity. For instance, I have this morning been cooking single-handedly for the brothers and guests in the monastery on a stifling day over a hot Aga! During the solitude period before afternoon manual work I have been able to bring my body and mind into a receptivity of calm and rest by the right posture and simple breathing exercises. As a result of this there is a letting-go of any build-up of tension, and a predisposition to meditative prayer. One can then move into the afternoon refreshed in body, mind and spirit, to deal not only with the manual and mental demands, but with the people who come for counselling, for retreat or to talk over their theological and spiritual reading.

Finding One's Own Posture

There is no particular posture which is suitable for all. Some brothers and sisters are able to adopt the 'perfect' cross-legged posture with little effort; others have spent months mastering it, while others find it a profitless exercise because of age, shape or conditioning! I find myself changing posture from time to time while favouring my prayer-stool. I am able to spend long periods in prayer and meditation lying on the floor on my back – it is virtually impossible for me to fall asleep in that position. The hard floor enables me to find the right relaxed posture and keeps my mind both at rest and alert. Sitting on a hard-backed chair or low stool, with straight back and feet firmly planted on the ground is ideal for some, while standing, or kneeling with face on the ground, or lying on one's tummy suits others. If one of the cross-legged postures is adopted a hard cushion or a low, home-made sitting stool is useful. My usual position is one of kneeling with the support of a prayer-stool. This posture has good ancestry, for we find that the New Testament makes kneeling symbolic of penitence, intercession, surrender and adoration. Jesus knelt to pray,[28] and so did Peter, Paul, and Stephen at his martyrdom.[29]

It is not difficult to construct a simple prayer stool. An illustrated diagram with measurements is given in the appendix or it can be purchased. The advantage of using one is that it is possible to retain a prayer-posture for an hour or more without discomfort. It is very difficult to stay within the stilled concentration of meditative or contemplative prayer if your legs have gone to sleep! The right posture is one which allows the circulatory system to function adequately and which does not induce sleepiness, and also does not put or keep the body under unnecessary strain. A straight back is universally recommended for long periods of meditation. All this implies that one is familiar, and in touch, with one's body.

Once a person starts on such a meditative path in which the body is taken up into prayer, all sorts of other questions arise, because we live in a world which is foreign to the New Testament. We suffer from obesity, the consumption of alcohol, nicotine, caffeine, chemically polluted instant foods. We lack exercise and manual work and need to simplify our sophisticated lifestyle. But keeping to our theme, let us now deal with the importance of breathing and body rhythm.

The Breath of God

It is significant that the Old Testament word for Spirit, *ruach*, is the same as that for wind or breath. The same holds for the New Testament Greek word *pneuma*. It is the same in the Sanskrit, and while giving a retreat at Malvern some time ago, the missionary sisters told me that it is also true of some of the African languages. The Spirit of God (*ruach Yahweh*), moved over the face of the waters at creation.[30] God breathed his life-giving *ruach* into Adam's nostrils and he became a living soul.[31] Reading the story of the valley of dry bones in Hebrew is an exercise in translation, for the wind, winds, breath and the Spirit are all derivatives of the one Hebrew word *ruach*.[32] When the risen Christ spoke his prophetic word to the band of believers, we read that He breathed on them and said: 'Receive the Holy Spirit.'[33] And when the Holy Spirit came in fulfilment of the promise we read that there came from heaven a sound like the rush of a mighty wind, filling the house, and they were all filled with the Holy Spirit (*pneumatos hagiou*).[34]

There is an intimate connection between breathing and the emotional life. I remember in my student days struggling through a rainy night, with a Norwegian friend, ahead of all the other international students, to plant the Welsh Dragon on the summit of the Rigi mountain in Switzerland. We did it, but reaching the top in the early morning, rain dispelled and rising sun glorious, we momentarily forgot the immediate task and became *breathless* with wonder at the panoramic view spread out before us. When we become excited, scared, or angry our breathing becomes short and rapid. When we are calm and gentle, in meditation or contemplation, the breath becomes slow, deep and rhythmic, and we become aware of our heartbeat.

If emotional, psychic states affect the breathing, it can also work the other way. Before an examination or interview (and now before preaching a sermon!), I would practise slow, deep breathing, with great calming effect.

This morning we said farewell to two young men who had come to find breathing space at our monastery. One of them is to be married in ten days' time, and he has slowed down his breathing and his life in preparation for the great day. The other came because of a hothouse religious pressure with its accompanying disenchantment, saying that 'prayer doesn't work'. We shared together in the very practice I have outlined, and from that experience emerged a dialogue of mind and heart that set his feet on the way to love in God again. We think somehow that we must pray with our brains and meditate with our mental processes. There is a form of meditation which is not illogical, but not merely rational. It is one in which there is a relaxed and calm posture, with deep, rhythmic breathing accompanying the heartbeat, and in which one is resting in the divine Love.

Only by practice can one realize and actualize the experience of the breath coming from the depths of one's being, opening up the areas of emotional and unconscious life within the presence and love of God. In the Bible the breath of man is a manifestation of the breath of Eternal Being, manifesting Itself also in the sighing of the wind, the roaring of the gales, and the gentle breeze of evening.

The regulation and awareness of one's own breathing brings one into an awareness and relationship with the cosmos. Our natural rhythms and physical elements are rooted in the earth. We are of dust and of heaven. The material stuff of earth and the breath of God constitute our natural, physical and spiritual being. This awareness of the body, its rhythm, heartbeat, breathing and posture is an awareness of the psychosomatic unity of the human person, preparing us for the practice of prayer and meditation in which God is encountered and experienced.

Experiment with Breathing
Now let's get some practice in. Repeat the posture practice – a quiet place, appropriate clothing, bare feet, your chosen posture – now relax. I shall suppose you are using a prayer-stool, and you are physically relaxed and free from physical tension.

Now note your breathing. Don't change it, just note it. Slowly control the rate of your breathing, make it rhythmic and regular, gently deepen it and slow it down. Be easy with yourself and establish a slow, deep, rhythmic pattern.

When the pattern is established and easy, try a simple exercise. Begin to count 'one' on the intake of breath – pause – and count 'two' on the outward breath. It will be strange at first, but gently persevere and it will establish itself:

1/pause/1,2
1/pause/1,2
1/pause/1,2

Do this for a few minutes, and if you are happy with it, you are ready for the next stage. If it is difficult, fall back into a quiet, rhythmic breathing at your own rate to go on to the next stage. The idea before going on is simply to breathe regularly, deeply, slowly, easily, and let yourself be carried deeper into yourself through breathing. It is natural, there is nothing to be frightened of, and it is all within the creative love of God, for the kingdom of God is within you.

Heartbeat
Now you are in this situation, you can go on with your eyes closed, half open, or open if it suits you. You may have the focus of attention such as a candle or an icon. This is often useful at the beginning until you leave it behind, as you enter more deeply into the awareness of your body rhythm.

Now you should be able to feel the pulsing of your heartbeat without need of actually taking your radial pulse. Follow this, linking it with your breathing, aware of the cosmic implication of breath and heartbeat, and the biblical teaching on the breath of God. This is not the time or place to set your logical process to work. It is the preparation for prayer, for resting in the divine Love.

Meditative Prayer
This is the point at which we may begin the Jesus Prayer which we deal with in chapter seven. But it is a preparation also for your own particular form of prayer or meditation. We have spoken of cosmic rhythm, and of the need for contemporary man to be in touch with himself, with his body and those parts of his psyche which are deprived in urban and technological life. The basic rhythms of earth and air, sea, sky and country, of changing seasons and physical labour in the fields are denied to most people. To have recourse to a simple method of being in touch with oneself, leading to psychical self-awareness and to the deeper levels of prayer in God, may be the beginnings of a new psychosomatic wholeness. Symptoms of neurotically based disease may be alleviated by such a practice, especially the kinds of afflictions that have a nervous basis, such as various skin ailments, stomach upsets with no organic cause, and anxiety symptoms leading to depression.

It is also true that a modified form of the above is suitable for those who are sick and feel that their powers of persistence and concentration are at a low ebb. When I visited our Somerset convent to celebrate the eucharist during the last year or two of Mother Agnes' life I used to take holy communion to her from the community celebration. After the blessing I used to stay and chat when she was able. A few months before she died she asked if I would obtain a Jesus Prayer rope and teach her the Jesus Prayer. I did this and we said the prayer together: 'Lord Jesus Christ, Son of God, have mercy on me, a sinner.' A little while afterwards, just before her death, she said to me, 'Brother, I can't remember the whole prayer, I just take hold of the rope (which she wore around her neck), and I repeat Jesus . . . Jesus . . . Jesus.'

It is also at this point in preparation that I have found, without effort or will, that I am singing in tongues, or become lost in sighing or groaning before God. There have been times when I have been drawn into a particular meditation, carried 'in the Spirit' to the mount of Transfiguration or to one of the healing miracles, to Gethsemane, or Calvary, or to the garden before the empty tomb.

If you find that God holds you in simple awareness and love at this point, don't move away. Stay with it, remain as long as He wants you to. If you are able, sing gently to Him or repeat familiar words of a hymn, a psalm or prayer. Often I have lingered in his presence, singing quietly for a time, and moving into silence.

In such periods of meditation you may begin to pray extemporaneously, or verbally bring into your prayer all the steps of your preparation:

My Father: You are nearer to me than breathing,
    closer than hands or feet;
Let me breathe the fragrance of your Spirit,
    and rejoice in the nearness of your presence

My Father: my heart beats in celebration of life;
    it pulses in the awareness of your love;
Grant that while my pulse and heartbeat remain
    I may love you, and then behold you in glory.

My Father: hold me closer to your heart of love,
   that I may feel the heartbeat of your passion;
May the loving kindness that fills your heart
   possess and unite me with yourself.

Centring Prayer

One of the simple exercises that Thomas Merton
commended is called Centring Prayer. The name is
newer than the method, and it bears a resemblance to
what we have advocated above, but its presentation is
simple.

   Merton is concerned to emphasize that prayer begins
not so much with the logical mind as with the believing
heart, the emphasis being on intuitive awareness of God.
It is a return to the heart, finding one's deepest centre,
awakening the profound depths of our being in the
presence of God who is the source of our being and of our
life. Centring Prayer is a method by which the believer
seeks to bring his scattered thoughts and feelings together
to allow for a certain deepening. The formulation of the
method is in three rules:

Rule One: We take a minute or two to quieten down
              and then move in faith to God dwelling in
our depths. At the end of the prayer we take several
minutes to come out, mentally praying the 'Our Father'
or some other prayer.
Rule Two: After resting for a while in the centre, in
              loving faith, we take a single, simple word
which expresses response to God (such as Abba, Father,
Maranatha, etc), and let it be present silently, repeating
itself as it will.
Rule Three: Whenever, in the continuity of the prayer,
               we become aware of anything else, we
simply, gently return to the Presence by the use of our
prayer word.

   In this way we may pass into a prayer of quiet
realization of God's loving presence. It is there we wish to

stay, in a state of loving attention, wholly centred on God, who is the heart of true prayer.

Creative Meditation

In this second part of the chapter on prayer and the body we shall be thinking of walking, dancing, and various creative activities of hand, heart, eye and mind, such as making music, calligraphy, bookbinding, writing poetry and keeping a journal. These are a selected group of meditative techniques which may be taken up into prayer, and which may serve as 'jumping off points' for a more contemplative way. There are, of course, many other creative techniques which have their meditative aspect and which may serve as channels in and through which the Holy Spirit may flow. This section may start you off in a new direction or may give impetus to some creative craft of which you have, up to now, failed to realize the spiritual potential.

Walking Meditation

The following chapter will be given to an Emmaus Walk, but there is another kind of walking meditation which is undertaken alone. It may be developed along one's own lines after some experimentation, but there are two versions which I use.

First there is the walking meditation which is linked to the Jesus Prayer and is included in that section. The second is the walk which has as its theme what may be called 'mindfulness' or 'insight'. It is the exercise of gentle concentration, while walking meditatively, that reaches out from within one's own depths, relating the inward to the outward, the immanent to the transcendent, and both in a mutuality in which one experiences the creative flow of the life of God in which we live and move and have our being.[35]

When the human quest is fulfilled in the revelation of God to the heart, there is effected what the Eastern Fathers called a *synergism*, a mutual working together of the human spirit and the Holy Spirit. This walk is a manifestation of such *synergism*. It is an awareness meditation in which there is a passive receptivity, a flowing out to meet whatever is presented, and an inflow of creativity that is a gift of grace.

The mechanics of the walk begin with the posture and relaxation exercise we outlined earlier with the prayer of invocation for the guidance of the Holy Spirit. As with walking the Jesus Prayer, there is the setting of the pace in a slow, measured walk, co-ordinated with deep but gentle belly breathing.

The idea of mindfulness or insight is the practice of becoming aware of oneself, one's environment, the weather, climate and solitude, integrating it all into the stuff of meditation. Suppose one is taking a walk in the early morning, just prior to the breaking of the dawn. First of all there is the sharp bite of early morning air, frost, or perhaps a stiff breeze. There is the first, stark, cold intake of breath and the accommodation of breathing, gait, and slow, steady, measured rate of walking.

As soon as one has mastered the meditative rhythm of limbs and body in movement and motion, then there is the awareness of the ground beneath one's feet, the texture of the grass or paving, or the firm softness of the sand. There is also the atmosphere of the early morning, the clear, crisp air, and the darkness giving way to streaks of morning light in the sky. Be aware! If there is a sunrise, what cosmic glory greets and enfolds you! I remember beautiful sunrises over the sea in the Gower Peninsula, and on dawn walks or jogging along Dorset lanes. And if the beauty of a calm or restless sea is part of the landscape, all this adds to the overall pattern of awareness, mindfulness and insight, within your own heart and in the world around you.

The object of this description is not to present it all on a plate, but to initiate you into such meditative walking, to encourage you to experiment with awareness, and to develop your own potentiality in observation, passive receptivity and mutuality with the created order.

Enoch walked with God into eternity; Noah walked

with God in uprightness; David walked with God in integrity of heart. And God's redeemed people are urged to walk on the highway of holiness with singing, joy and gladness, where sorrow and sighing shall flee before them.[36]

In such walking meditations I have found great variety. There have been times when my inward mood has answered to the light, darkness, mists or sunshine that has greeted me. And there have been times when the mood, climate or terrain has dictated the direction of the meditation. I have already referred to the way in which the Island of Bardsey off the Lleyn Peninsula appears to have moods of its own, and one is often caught up into the glory or mystery of the night or morning in its shadow.

I have maintained that this walk is undertaken alone. Of course it is possible to do such an awareness walking meditation with a friend, but the quality of trust and friendship should be such as can bear silence, reflection and mutually co-ordinated movement. And this is not easy.

Walking meditation is simple and easy – but very difficult! It is difficult or impossible if one looks at it as an achievement, but simple and beautiful if one is childlike, open and receptive to whatever comes. Don't set out with preconceived notions, just experiment and develop your own style. There may well be opportunities sometimes to share and explore the dimension with another. If so, then do that. But for a couple or a group, the Emmaus Walk may be more appropriate.

Dancing

It is quite clear that the Christian is committed to exercising his body as well as stimulating his mind and extending the horizons of his spirit. When the apostle wrote: 'bodily exercise profits a little', he was comparing it with godliness which is profitable for all things,[37] and was not discouraging physical exercise. He took his own analogies from the games, the gymnasium and the marathon of the day.[38]

We are encouraged to lay aside all hindrances to the race, and to run with patience, looking to Jesus our true forerunner, for we are surrounded by the great cloud of witnesses which is the communion of saints.[39] And all this links appropriately with the physical body and the regenerate spirit being the temple of the Holy Spirit, who calls us to purity and wholeness.

We have included a chapter on the physical and meditative aspects of jogging, aware of the fact that not a great number of our readers may be able to embark on such a demanding practice (though it is not to be dismissed on the grounds of age, laziness or sloth!). But here we shall consider dance. Dancing to or before the Lord is part of Old Testament worship and practice,[40] and it is refreshing to find its restoration in worship in both the catholic and evangelical sections of the Church.

At a great Missionary eucharist at St. Mary's Cathedral, Glasgow, a few years ago, we invited members of the Community of Celebration to come and share their music and liturgical dance with us. There was certain suspicion among some members of choir and congregation beforehand, but all were won over by the sheer beauty, reverence, sense of worship and joy of the liturgical dance which was performed by the young people with a background of wind and string instruments and finger cymbals, as they danced a Jewish melody in place of the Gradual hymn.

Recently I shared in a 'Communities Day' in Dorset when all the local communities got together for their annual celebration and sharing. One of the workshops was on 'Sacred Dance', and there we were put through our paces, with gospel exposition of each dance that we were taught. One I found great fun was called 'Ruach' which, as we have seen, is the Hebrew word for breath, wind or spirit. And because the Society of Saint Francis was one of the communities represented, the Sacred Dance Group danced and mimed the St. Francis' prayer: 'Lord, make me an instrument of your peace'.

As we learned there, there are opportunities for young

and old, fat and thin, active and slothful, to dance to the Lord. It is surprising that people who know themselves not to be young, slim, lithe, athletic and graceful, can enter into the grace and movement of dance with a new sense of rhythm and freedom of worship which may liberate other areas of mental and spiritual life, as well as setting them free from all kinds of British reserve and inhibition.

I am a beginner in all this, but I have developed for myself certain forms of charismatic and aerobic dance in which I sometimes 'limber up' for prayer in the mornings, or just dance before the Lord in a personally choreographed or completely spontaneous manner, according to the mood of the moment and the music which I sometimes use.

When I spent three weeks with the Anchorhold Community in East Sussex I shared with the members every day in their physical and meditation exercises, which often included dance and movement which was prescribed and guided with selected music. This is the kind of meditation form I hope to develop as a corporate exercise with the novices who spend nine months of their learning noviciate in our Glasshampton monastery, for instruction in silence, prayer and the more contemplative side of their lives.

Once launched in this dimension, I have found great joy in developing my own forms. There is an excellent recreation room in our Dorset friary which is used for groups and pantomimes! It is spacious, carpeted and sometimes warm, and is ideal for dance and aerobic exercise. Aerobic exercise may take many forms, e.g., jogging, cycling, swimming, dancing – indeed any activity which gets the heart beating faster, accompanied by the breathlessness that comes from moderate to demanding exercise. I would add all the usual cautions about moderation, not starting quickly, not exceeding one's limits and so on. But I would still commend it.

As to my own methods. The more formal movements are geared to trinitarian forms and symbols which are evocative of the incarnation, mighty works, passion and resurrection of Jesus. I do not have written forms but plan them before I enact them. They are regulated and symbolic movements more than dance. These are not necessarily done to music, though some of the forms are enhanced by such meditative mood music as Bruch's *Kol Nidri* cello music or the *Agnus Dei* from Bach's B minor mass.

Then there are the spontaneous, unchoreographed joyful dances to the Lord which are entered into for sheer joy of creation and redemption, and almost any music from 'Christian' to 'pop' is used here – though, of course, one is selective. At the beginning of this section I mentioned various publications and video programmes one can hire-purchase to demonstrate such group and personal aerobic and dance forms as preparation to prayer or to Bible study.

Creative Meditation

The previous section may not be everyone's style for all kinds of reasons, so let me turn to more gentle creative crafts and exercises which may be done in the spirit of prayer or may lead into a deeper realization of God's loving presence. I call this area 'creative meditation' because I find that the creativity involved and the concentration demanded is fulfilled in what the old teachers of prayer called 'recollection'. This is an expression of the spirituality found in Brother Lawrence's *The Practice of the Presence of God*.[41]

Music Making

Sadly, I am not a musician, but my two periods of solitude caused me to take up my recorder and use it in my periods of meditation. There was one day, when after midday office, I sat in the doorway of my hut and gently played the recorder to the Lord. It is difficult to describe the breathtaking beauty of the tree-covered hillside which ascended from the deep valley in which my hut was situated in Dorset. Such was the valley that sound echoed and re-echoed, and up in the top hut-hermitage one of our other brothers was spending his few days' retreat. He told me later that he had just come to the end of some very moving reading, when he heard wafting up from the valley below the sounds of a recorder playing John Ireland's setting:

My song is love unknown,
My Saviour's love to me,
Love to the loveless shown,
That they might lovely be.
  O who am I
  That for my sake
  My Lord should take
  Frail flesh, and die.

There are numerous references in Scripture, and especially in the psalms to praising God corporately on various instruments of music[42] as was doubtless practised in the second temple, and also the personal taking up of an instrument to meditate or to praise the Lord, with wind, string or percussion. When novices come to Glasshampton monastery for their months of 'learning to be quiet'[43] it is interesting to see the creative things they take up which enrich their interior life. Some bring a guitar, a recorder, a tin whistle, and after supper they will sometimes retire to the corner tower where they cannot be heard, and strum or play, sometimes together, sometimes alone, until Compline.

During my long periods of solitude, after eucharist and breakfast, I would devote the whole Sunday morning to intercessory prayer. This was when I would take my list of 500 people (!) and bring them to the Lord. They would all be named, but I would divide them into sections of twenty, and would find myself lingering over particular names. Often between the sections I would play a hymn of worship, intercession or penitence on their behalf, or in praise for and with the person(s) for whom I was praying. Many people do this sort of thing without realizing that they are participating in a valid form of adoration and intercessory prayer, using mind, heart, tongue, hands, feet and whatever! With me this sometimes gives way to laying aside the instrument and the prayer list, and falling on my face in love and worship.

Music lifts the hearts of many to communion with and in God. St. Augustine said that he who sings prays twice. The making of such music in playing and singing in the vernacular, in Latin, (as in some of the contemporary Taize settings of Scripture and prayer[44]) and in the gift of tongues, is an experience of deepening prayer. There is no need for me to do more than refer to the use of music in meditation in drawing attention to some of the great mass settings, instrumental and choral works, which have always been recognized as inspired and inspiring. The *Update* magazine referred to earlier promotes modern 'Christian pop' and folk music side by side with traditional Latin plainchant from the monks of Prinknash Abbey – *Spiritus Domini*, *Veni Creator Spiritus*, *Ave Verum Corpus*, *Salve Regina*, and English Plainsong settings from the Jerusalem Bible. To find a basically evangelical magazine including such material is refreshing.

I have spent many hours expounding, and then listening prayerfully to, Elgar's *Dream of Gerontius* with three groups of contemplative nuns, and friars of our own Order. The poetry of John Henry Newman so perfectly wedded to Elgar's setting intensifies the heights and depths of the theological and devotional material that one is drawn into that borderland between meditation and contemplation. In such a state one is taught by the Spirit and caught up in response to a theology which is mystical in its form and content.

Heredity and training, environment and temperament all affect one's response to particular music. Not everyone will warm to Bach's B minor mass, and not everyone will experience the intellectual and aesthetic satisfaction felt by some when listening to Bach's forth-eight Prelude and Fugue form studies in his *Well Tempered Clavier* collection. What to some people would be ideal meditative music would be a certain distraction to others. But what might begin as a penance in being exposed to Bach's *St Matthew Passion* with a prayer-group during Lent, could become a profound experience of entering into the darkness and glory of Calvary.

Calligraphy

A simple art form which I have found productive in terms of a meditative technique is calligraphy. There are, of course, many forms of artistic lettering and much literature on the subject. The recently published material on Chinese calligraphy alone is both enormous and baffling. I will confine my comments to attempts at mastery of the italic hand. I have recently read, with much pleasure, pieces of beautiful prose concerning brushes, quills, nibs, sandalwood and perfumed inks of Japanese, Chinese and Indian origin – and whether one should rub one's own ink or be more philistine and use a commercial ink fluid. These are concerns for the purist, but I shall just be concerned with a good quality black fountain-pen ink for disposable lettering and an Indian ink for permanent lettering and the inscribing of books.

Let me illustrate my own use of the technique as a way of praying. I lay out my materials on a table, with a firm seat at the right height. Then I spend some time with the posture/relaxation/centring practice described earlier. When I feel ready, I gently commit myself to God by saying the *Gloria*, or some ascription of praise and trust, and sit down before the calligraphy materials. One of the things I have done recently is to slowly reproduce in the italic hand about fifty selected sayings from *The Book of the Lover and the Beloved*, by the 13th century Franciscan Ramon Lull. The very copying of these contemplative sayings is a means of being gently drawn into prayer and love, expressing the deepest relationship between the soul and God as Lover and Beloved. The sayings contain elements of the great mystic way of purgation, illumination and union, and an hour or two spent in such an exercise fires one's mind and heart with the love of God and neighbour.

One can write out the Office of Compline, one of the epistles of St John, a group of poems from the metaphysical poets, or prepare an anthology of one's favourite quotations. In my case this led to the desire to make and bind my own books, and that is the next meditative practice I want to suggest.

Bookbinding
Patience and concentration are required to learn simple bookbinding techniques, but it is sheer joy to take up the results of one's calligraphy, e.g. fifty or one hundred pages of three-coloured italic reproductions of the sayings of Ramon Lull on the life of prayer, and bind them into an attractive book for one's own devotional use, or for presentation to a friend.

Just as one can easily obtain 'know-how' books on calligraphy, so one can learn bookbinding from well-presented instructions, though like the life of prayer, it is infinitely better to have a teacher and guide. I shall not spend time therefore on know-how or materials, save to say that PVA glue, a sample wallpaper book, a Stanley knife, a press, and an assortment of cloth material scraps will set you up for simple jobs.

The point I am obviously making is that as I repair and refurbish our Bibles, hymn books, psalters, and library books, I enter more deeply into meditative prayer and recollection in much the same way as the desert fathers of the third and fourth centuries plaited their baskets to the glory of God and to support themselves. And they said the Jesus Prayer as they worked with their hands. I'm sure St Paul did much the same thing as he applied himself to his tent-making. It is also wise to be modest in one's endeavours, it is not necessary to produce illuminated Latin manuscript work on vellum, bound in leather and tooled in gold leaf, to fulfil the requirements of simple manual work and accompanying prayer!

Keeping a Journal
Closely allied to the copying and making of books is the

practice of keeping a journal. The recording of one's spiritual quest and pilgrimage, the marking of milestones, the recalling and recording of days of emptiness or splendour – all these can serve to deepen one's relationship with God in prayer and love. Such a task is like the sharing of love letters. The dimensions of the loved one's mind and heart are opened up to you, as yours are opened up to him or her. This is both a discipline and a joy, for you soon find yourself in dialogue with God as well as with your own soul. Not only will you find yourself writing truthfully about yourself at a depth unknown previously, but you will find an almost prophetic emergence of the will of God for your life as it unfolds before you in your journal. And even if this is not transparently evident, you will certainly find that the answers to some of your deepest emotional and spiritual difficulties will be implicit in the way you state the problem.

This journal is not to be an adolescent diary, but a journal of spiritual pilgrimage. It need not be kept daily or even weekly, but perhaps twice or three times a month, or when a matter of importance, difficulty, or illumination arises, then more frequently. It can also be used in conjunction with your spiritual reading or with questions posed by your spiritual director or soul-friend. You will also see how valuable such a journal can be when shared with friends who have a mutual bond of pilgrimage in the life of prayer. I take this matter up later in dealing with a corporate group meeting in which such sharing of a journal kept in 'hut retreats' is part of the discipline of prayer.

A young man recently came to the monastery for a few days declaring that he had lost his faith and had no sense of direction or meaning in his life. On the first evening he presented me with the journal he had kept of his opinions, feelings and problems. I took the journal, shared and prayed with him on the first evening and told him to go to bed early and have a lie-in in the morning. So we met at 10.30 am, and on the basis of what he had written we entered into areas of thinking, feeling and praying which were new to him, but were implicit in the stating of his thoughts in the journal. The journal was a real asset in dealing with the actual problems he was facing. It saved me answering questions which he was not asking!

We shall refer to the Book of Psalms as illustrating periods of what we may call 'experimental theology' in the section on Prayer and the Word of God; suffice it to say here that the psalmist actually records his personal and corporate feelings about joy and grief, ecstasy and abandonment, and breaks out into lament or praise as the occasion arises – and writes in all down! The Gospels certainly were the spiritual journal *par excellence* of the four evangelists, and the epistles bear record of inner spiritual illumination. St Luke did well to dedicate his two spiritual journals (the Gospel and the Acts) to the most noble Theophilus, whoever he may have been.

There are many autobiographies which trace a psychical and spiritual pilgrimage. The proto-type in modern 'confessional' style is the classic work of St Augustine which only has to be read slowly and prayerfully to enable one to see how the writing of experienced truth clarifies one's own mind, and leads the heart into integrity and love. What beautiful writing this is:

Too late loved I Thee, O Thou Beauty of ancient days, yet ever new! too late I loved Thee! And behold, Thou wert within, and I abroad, and there I searched for Thee; deformed I, plunging amid those fair forms, which Thou hadst made. Thou wert with me, but I was not with Thee. Things held me far from Thee, which, unless they were in Thee, were not at all. Thou calledst, and shoutedst, and burstest, my deafness. Thou flashedst, shonest, and scatteredst my blindness. Thou breathedst odours, and I drew in breath and pant for Thee. I tasted, and hunger and thirst. Thou touchedst me, and I burned for Thy peace.[45]

Get an exercise book then, spend a little time in

quietness before God in the fashion we have recommended, and reflect on your new thinking about prayer, pilgrimage and the simplification of your own life in God:

Saturday, 7th May, 19--:
After hearing a talk about prayer and the body on Thursday, I decided to have a go this morning. I was distracted and all over the place and couldn't hold my concentration at all. The fellow talked about awareness – all I was aware of was the novelty of it all, and the strange, slow measured tread I was supposed to initiate. I think I was trying too hard!
Saturday, 21st May, 19--:
I think I've made something of a discovery! It isn't anything revolutionary, but simply that somehow the Jesus Prayer is working. I didn't get on with the walking with it, but I've fixed up a prayer corner in my bedroom with an icon, a candle and a Bible. I have just tried a few sessions over the last fortnight before going to bed and something's happening inside. I don't know quite what it is, but it feels positive and good, and something like what I think prayer should be. I think I need to find a group which practises this prayer, and talk to someone who knows about it.

Writing Poetry
There are, of course, many creative areas in which one can use hand, mind and heart together. Within our own community brothers make sandals, habits, prayer-stools, do woodcarving, paint and mount icons, and even cook and grow vegetables meditatively! All these are good in themselves, and are conducive to recollected prayer. But before we conclude this section there is one other practice which is more widespread than it appears and which is productive in recording and stimulating dimensions of meditation – and that is the writing of something which resembles poetry. I am not speaking of writing for

publication. The results of such work may mean nothing to anyone but yourself, but that's all right. Some of the best writing, in poetry and prose has been that which has been written as a result of an inward compulsion, and certainly not to satisfy the whims of an audience!

Many young men and women have taken up their pens in the first flush of a new love, and written reams of doggerel if one were to judge it objectively. But that is not the canon of judgment. What I have said in regard to keeping a journal holds for the most part, in writing poetry. Certainly one will not write poetry of any depth unless one loves and has read some of the great poets. It is not a matter of scribbling one's thoughts when spring is in the air and breaking into rhyming couplets! A study of, for instance, the metaphysical poetry of John Donne will soon dispel the illusion that the writing of poetry is 'easy' or that it has to do with an elusive inspiration and little to do with discipline, intellectual energy, and the ability to communicate the substance of heart and mind.

But the above paragraph has to do with the discipline of poetry, and I am really concerned with the unique joy that comes with the ability to feel, catch and communicate the experiences of the heart and the flashes of intellectual inspiration that illuminate the mind. I am writing in the context of meditation and prayer, and concrete expressions of what I mean can be seen in the best kind of religious verse, and in the classic theological and devotional hymns of the Church. But beware, for some of the material, even in the *Oxford Book of Mystical Verse* is, to say the least, unworthy, and some of the hymns even of men like Charles Wesley and Isaac Watts reveal that inspiration was not always running high!

Nevertheless, to commit the stuff of meditation to verse, and to reduce, polish and finish it is an exercise in prayer and clarity. Like the writing of a journal it opens up areas of one's own heart and mind which are sometimes hidden and gives further impetus to enquiry and research. The prose and poetry that people write in times of great love or grief, in extreme sickness or when under threat, persecution or imprisonment are revealing not only to themselves, but as sources of inspiration and strength to those who have never descended to such places of height of depth. One only has to think of the blazing poetry of St John of the Cross written in the cramped darkness of his prison cell, the pilgrimage to the celestial city from the Bedford gaol of John Bunyan, or in more recent times the *Letters and Papers from Prison* of Dietrich Bonhoeffer, Richard Wurmbrand, or the diary of Anne Frank.

The stuff of dreams and the awareness of the mystery of God given in certain times of prayer cannot easily be captured in prose, and evades verbal communication, but can occasionally find expression in free or metred verse form. If I illustrate this by one simple experience from a cold, rainy winter's day on the Lleyn Peninsula it will convey both the substance and the feeling of that afternoon.

It had been raining all day. I had made sure that my water supply was in, and had spent most of the day in prayer, study and bookbinding. The rain lashed against the walls and small windows of the cottage by the wind. Because it was dark and menacing, I had a small light on the broad window-sill which looked out on to a sloping grassy area. That kind of day causes me to enter more deeply into myself and sigh for the Love which is the source of all. I stopped my work for some moments and looked out of the tiny window. There, huddled against the low wall, windswept and soaked by the rain, stood a yearling lamb. It is not always easy to know at such times whether the moments of vision well up entirely from within oneself, or whether there is something objectively clear in the separate pieces that go to make up the whole scene.

However that may be, I was seized in those moments with such a vision of the symbolism of the Lamb of God in its gentleness, innocence, sacrifice, obedience and patience, that I was brought to tears. The great scriptural words set firmly into the eucharist sounded in my mind and heart:

Agnus Dei, qui tollis peccata mundi,
  miserere nobis;
Agnus Dei, qui tollis peccata mundi,
  dona nobis pacem.

Lamb of God, who takes away the sins of the world,
  have mercy on us;
Lamb of God, who takes away the sins of the world,
  grant us peace.

I sat down, in the midst of the experience, quietly wept in the presence and love of God, and simply had to write to communicate to myself just what I felt about such a beautiful and penetrating experience of sadness, wonder and love. The poem is included in the appendix.

Afterwards I sang quietly the little childhood song which I had loved, 'All in the April evening', which itself speaks of the silence, suffering and passion of Jesus the Lamb. And I repeated William Blake's 'Little lamb, who made thee', which has always been a favourite. But most of all I returned to the poem which enshrined the experience, and just stayed there for a long time.

This section on the body and creative meditation is meant to act as a stimulus to your own experimentation. Many manual crafts can be turned into contemplative awareness, and can provide pools of receptivity in which the loving and creative presence of God may be tasted and enjoyed.

Reflections on Jogging

We have made a case for a Christian to be physically and mentally in good shape. 'Shape up!' is good advice for the body as well as the soul! Some time ago I published an article on jogging which brought me letters and comments from young and old, and started many people on the jogging path. Since that time, I have discussed the points made in various young people's groups and have found fruitful dialogue with those who are getting body and soul together in the way of prayer. I reproduce the substance of that article as it makes its own statement:

Reflections on Jogging
It's Sunday afternoon at Glasshampton monastery, and
I've just returned after an hour's jogging, down the track,
over the fields, on to the road, up to the 'Rose and
Crown' (no, I didn't go in!) and back again. I've come
out of the shower and now have that wonderful feeling of
being tired and clean, just in the mood to write about this
popular but precarious practice of jogging.

Back in June I used to go jogging at 6.00 am on alter-
nate mornings, over the track, through the fields, down to
the lake and back before morning prayer and eucharist.
At present it's dark and very muddy at that time, and
complicated by the fact that the late beet crop is being
hauled in and the tractor has made the first 300 yards like
a quagmire! So I get out when I can. But what a joy it is!

The first thing I feel when jogging is the awareness of
the complementary of *discipline* and *spontaneity*. At
6.00 am, or even now after morning prayer and eucharist
at 8.15 am, the bleak coldness and icy wind of a winter
morning in vest and shorts does not always invite one to
plunge out with great enthusiasm – but always, within
minutes, there is the exhilaration of movement, slight
breathlessness and flooding warmth – if you keep going!
To respond in spontaneity when the sun rises in
Worcestershire splendour in the wide sky on an early
June morning is glorious, but to live under the same
discipline on a cold wintry morning at the turn of the year
evokes the spontaneity, now hard-earned, but doubly
rewarding, confirming the discipline-spontaneity polarity
in other areas of life.

Then there is the joyful discovery of the union of
physicality and *spirituality*. 'Brother Ass', as St Francis
called the body, is a stubborn but faithful friend. To be at
home in the body is essential to good jogging and good
faith. I must listen to my physicality, be gentle and loving
with my whole self, and certainly with my body. Jogging
is not competitive, it is not cross-country running, it is not

going hard at it and becoming exhausted. No, it is a gentle but firm jogging pace which makes me aware of my rhythm, of my heartbeat, of my respiration, of the harmony and movement that underlines the unity of body, mind and spirit. It enables me towards the full acceptance of my physicality, of my sexuality, of the need to let the mind and spirit guide, while listening to the body in sensory awareness of the created order.

There are times, of course, when I get the sudden urge to do a sprint, and break all the jogging rules which are wisely and cautiously set out for the over 25s! Then comes the terrific surge of challenge and exhilaration, the pounding of the blood, the increase of the heartbeat, the panting and sweating as Brother Ass protests and rebukes the charioteer! Jogging experts – please don't write and tell me how wrong this is – I know – but I still do it! And I'm not asking anyone to emulate me.

Then there is the *finitude-immortality* polarity which I often feel as I jog along, all too aware that I am not as fit as I was, or as I ought to be. I cannot do what once I could, and I hear my body telling me not to make too heavy a demand. I remember the days when I would cycle the 60-odd miles from Swansea to Cardigan on a Friday evening after work, and back again at 5.00 am on Monday morning to get into work at 9.00 am and be full of joy and exuberance on the Monday evening. Those days are gone! But I am still aware of the goodness of the body, of my basic acceptance of my physicality, and of the fact that I rejoice in the Hebraic tradition of the resurrection of the body.

I do not know the nature of the resurrection body, but a body it will be! I mean that it will be fashioned upon the model of our Lord's transfiguration and resurrection, and there will be a tangibility and a physicality which will be spiritual, and transfigured in such a manner as is beyond my comprehension, but which will be the principle of the divinisation or theosis of the whole cosmos. I don't say that I shall be jogging in heaven, but the analogy transposed is mind-blowing! My body joins my mind and spirit and cries, 'Even so, come, Lord Jesus!'

There is, of course, the awareness of 'change and decay in all around I see' – that my present body, though good and wholesome, is finite and subject to mortality and decay. My medical training served to make this clear, and pastoral experience only underlined the sadness of our mortal state, with the accompanying Christian joy of acceptance of mortality and 'sister death'. In one sense, death of the body is a friend to the Christian who understands the principle of the seed falling into the ground to die; but where death is seen as the great enemy, we rejoice in Jesus the Saviour who overcame death by His own death and resurrection.

This brings me to the pattern of prayer and response in my periods of jogging. It draws together the understanding of both the *transcendence* and the *immanence* of God, the complete otherness, and the present immediacy of his divine indwelling. There are times when the glory of rising or setting sun (depending on the time of day!), or the radiance or bleakness of the day, fills me with a sense of the utter otherness of God. The flight of wild geese, the friendly cows and horses, the silence and solitude of the countryside in early morning – all these things cause me to cry out to God in song and praise – or to feel the subdued silence of his glory. As I feel upsurging response to the revelation of God in nature, I realize the splendour of the indwelling Spirit, the mystical Christ with whom and in whom I live and move and have my being. This is true quite apart from the incarnation of our Lord, but it is because of that incarnation, passion and resurrection that I can fully enter into such a blinding awareness of God manifest in nature, manifest in the flesh, and manifest in me!

All this is quite independent of variation in mood with which I shall conclude in a moment. There is something about prayer in the context of jogging that assures me of the great objective Being and work of God in creation and redemption. It is an experience which I enjoy for its own sake, but which cannot help but cause such experiential reflections as I have written here.

Then variation of *moods* and *constancy*. Thomas Merton says somewhere that when you feel dispirited and full of *accidie* (listlessness), you should go out into the fields, get your hands into the soil, or sweat a bit in manual labour, and this will bring you into physical and spiritual receptivity in which God can give you an intuition or consciousness of himself. This is so with jogging too! There is something about the discipline, the rhythm, the getting together of the physical and the spiritual, the pounding heart, the panting breath, and the gentle challenge to the body that brings one into interior silence to match the exterior solitude. The mood is deepened or transfigured often corresponding to the appropriate changing of the seasons. It may be that sadness is deepened and spiritualized, or joy becomes ecstatic and turns into a charismatic dance in the middle of a cornfield, or silence and peace take possession, and I lie down in the grass in adoration of God.

There is more – so much more – some that cannot be written. And Jesus runs with me – and I with him – and within me, and above me, and below me, and on before me into the Glory. So, 'Let us lay aside every weight, and the sin which clings so closely, and let us run with perseverence in the race that is set before us, looking to Jesus, the Pioneer and Perfector of our faith . . .'.[46]

That is where the article ended. There is now a growing number of people who have made jogging part of their prayer discipline. One of the older theological students who often stays at the friary is one of these. He has given up teaching to be ordained, with the pressure of studies for ordination as well as a busy life as a husband and father. He maintains that jogging three times a week is a refreshing release from mounting academic demands, making him more able to cope. Another two married friends, to the amusement of their wives at first, meet a few times a week in the early morning for their jogging sessions before work. My response to them was: 'Why don't your wives join you too?' They are now working on that!

Just in case you feel that jogging is not your particular style, why not take seriously the suggestions made in the next chapter which is concerned with an Emmaus Walk?

References

 1 Cor. 6:20
 2 Heb. 10:5
 3 Rom. 7:14–25
 4 Eph. 5:29
 5 Eph. 1:10,20–23
 6 Exod. 34:29–35; Acts 6:15; Luke 9:28–36
 7 Eph. 1:14; 4:30
 8 2 Cor. 4:16
 9 1 Thess. 5:23
10 Eph. 5:23
11 1 Cor. 3:16
12 Rom. 12:1
13 1 Cor. 12:12–31
14 1 Thess. 5:23
15 1 Cor. 15:51ff.
16 2 Cor. 4:7–12
17 Phil. 3:21
18 Ps. 139:2,3
19 Pss. 1:1; 150:4; 95:6; 1 Cor. 14:25
20 The magazine referred to is a new publication called
      Christian Update. The Bible Society's book is:
      Lamont, Gordon, *Move Yourselves*, Swindon:
      (Bible Society, 1983).
21 1 Thess. 4:11
22 Pss. 4:4; 46:10
23 Mark 5:34; Matt. 11:28
24 Matt. 14:13,23; 17:1; Mark 6:31; Luke 6:12
25 Matt. 4:1–11 and parallels
26 Matt. 6:6
27 Mark 8:34

28 Luke 22:41
29 Acts 9:40; 20:36; 7.60
30 Gen. 1:2
31 Gen. 2:7
32 Ezek. 37:1–14
33 John 20:22
34 Acts 2:2, 4
35 Acts 17:28
36 Isa. 35:8–10
37 1 Tim. 4:8
38 1 Cor. 9:24–27
39 Heb. 12:1, 2
40 Exod. 15:20; Jer. 31:13; Pss. 30:11; 149:3; 150:4; 2 Sam. 6:14
41 Brother Lawrence, *The Practice of the Presence of God*, London: Burns & Oates (1977).
42 e.g. Ps. 150
43 1 Thess. 4:11
44 Cf. the liturgical publications of the Taize Community, especially the international and ecumenical musical settings
45 *The Confessions of Saint Augustine*, Bk. X (XXVI), 37. London: J. M. Dent (1967)
46 Hebrews 12:1, 2

5: An Emmaus Walk

An Emmaus Walk is a walking meditation which is done with another person. I introduced it a few years ago as a post-Easter exercise for our friars and sisters, and it has since spread to churches, schools, prayer groups and retreatants with some enthusiasm. It is simple, biblical, and has the virtue of providing both input and feedback. I shall describe it simply, and then include the original pattern which has been used as a basis for such a walk.

One and a half or two hours are needed for this walk, inclusive of the time spent together before and after the exercise. A whole group can meet together for the first section, breaking up into pairs for the walk, and there may be a general coming together after the walk at an agreed time to pool experiences. If this is part of a group exercise, it would have to be planned carefully. It would be a better plan in such a case to begin together, but to arrange a separate evening to meet for the pooling of experiences. I shall outline it as for our own community, assuming its use for two people.

1 Introduction
'Did not our hearts burn within us while he talked with us on the road, and while he opened to us the Scriptures.'
Two people meet in a quiet place. After settling into a relaxed silence, they pray and read as follows:
a. Invocation: (the following, or an extempore prayer)
LORD JESUS CHRIST: Grant us now a sense of your living presence, and by the light of your Holy Spirit open our minds to your love. As the hearts of the Emmaus walkers burned within them so long ago, so may your loving presence be the source of warmth and light to us as

we walk with you and reflect on your word. And to you be thanks and praise, in the glory of the Father and the unity of the Holy Spirit. Amen.

b. Scripture: (read audibly one of the following, or any chosen passage)

Luke 24: 13–35   The Emmaus Walk
Matt. 4: 1–11   The Temptation of Jesus
Matt. 4: 18–25   Call and Healing
Matt. 5: 1–14   Jesus' Teaching
Matt. 5: 38–48   The Way of Love

Appropriate to Lent/Passiontide

Matt. 26: 31–35;   Peter's Denial (on return read
  69–75   John 21: 15–19)
Matt. 26: 36–56   Gethsemane and the Arrest of
                             Jesus
Matt. 27: 11–31   The Trial and Mocking of Jesus
Matt. 27: 32–56   The Crucifixion and Death of
                             Jesus

Some modern translations supply a table of the parables and miracles of our Lord. Almost any such passage is suitable for meditative reading at this point.

c. Commentary on the reading, poetry, etc.
d. Five minutes of shared silence.

2. The Walk

a. The route should have been planned and 'walked' previously. The outward walk should take at least half an hour, and the aim should be a prayerful sharing on the basis of the Scripture/commentary read, with freedom to move into other areas if led.

b. When the outward point has been reached, the pair should pause, turn and begin to retrace their steps together, but now in silence. There should be an openness of heart and mind to the Lord and one another, in simple awareness of our Lord's promised presence.

3. Conclusion

a. Return to the quiet place.

b. If desired, re-read the Scripture or the second part of the agreed passage, (e.g. if Peter's denial has been read, then Peter's confession of love for Christ can now be read).

c. Spend at least a further five minutes in silence.

d. Collect and Grace:

LORD JESUS CHRIST: We thank you for your presence with us on our pilgrimage, for our time together and for all we have received from your hand. Enable us to carry your healing presence to our brothers and sisters, and ever to walk with you, until the day of your appearing, in the glory of the Father, and the unity of the Holy Spirit. Amen.

THE GRACE of our Lord Jesus Christ, and the love of God, and the fellowship of the Holy Spirit be with us evermore. Amen.

The Emmaus Walk exercise is meant to provide a simple way of sharing with another something of the experience which occurred on the road to Emmaus so long ago. In order to be silent with another there needs to be a great measure of trust and openness. Only in a relationship of such loving trust can be presence of Christ manifest itself in a quality of fellowship not previously experienced. When this happens there is immense joy – and sometimes profound wonder.

But a warning note needs to be sounded. This Walk must not be undertaken lightly without due preparation and prayer. Silence in solitude or shared with another can expose a person to the light and scrutiny of God, and the result could be either a sense of fear at being so exposed, or an experience of embarrassment and the inability to share, or to cope.

If prayerful preparation has been undertaken, and the first experience doesn't altogether succeed, don't let that worry you. There is a novelty-factor that has to be worked through, and temperamental differences to be allowed for. Persistence, and allowing for one another is part of this exercise. One grows into shared silence, and what began as a novelty, or as an embarrassing non-verbal walk can turn out to be a fruitful sharing of a love which transcends human friendship and participates in the divine Love.

6: Prayer and the Word of God

The power of Scripture in conversion and in the life of prayer is consistently illustrated in the lives of the saints. In the third century as a young man, Antony of Egypt heard Scripture read in the mass in such a way that it became God's word to him to sell his possessions and live the life of prayer in the wilderness. There was struggle and conflict but his victorious life became the model and inspiration of the whole monastic tradition. In the fourth century, Augustine, after spending youthful years of searching and speculation, heard God's word as a distinct call to Christ for cleansing and holiness. And in the thirteenth century, when Francis Bernadone with two friends went to church to hear the Gospel read, they were given clear direction from Scripture and were thrust out to pioneer the great Franciscan way of living gospel simplicity and poverty, saturated with prayer and joyful adoration of God.

Scripture encourages us to pray fervently, unceasingly and persistently,[1] and the word of God in Scripture is the very life-blood of men and women of prayer. The Church has always held Scripture as its treasure and is always under its judgment. The most unchurchly characters, the old desert fathers who fled from a worldly Constantinian church, clung tenaciously to Scripture and psalms. Indeed, the revelation of God often came to people in the desert, on the lone mountain, in caves and in the wilderness. Solitude and prayer is the cradle of Scripture, and Scripture begets people of prayer.

'Come ye yourselves apart' is the word of Christ in the New Testament, whether it be to a solitary place for refreshment and teaching, or up to the mountain of Transfiguration for a revelation of glory when, 'apart, by themselves alone' they saw no one but Jesus only. But always there is the confrontation of the soul with the word of God.

Praying Scripture

Scripture is the staple diet of the person of prayer, and there are many ways of considering its truth. We are not here concerned with a critical approach to Scripture, though that has its indispensable place in theological study. The uncritical acceptance of the Bible has given rise to bloodshed, hatred, crusades and bigotry that have often turned the honest humanist away in disgust, not to mention the mushrooming of heresies and sects based on a 'private' reading of Scripture. Scripture must be read in and with the Church led by the Holy Spirit.[2] The genuine mystic and contemplative has always kept the spirit of the canon of catholicity respecting the fundamentals of the Faith, '*quod semper, quod unique, quod ab omnibus*' those things which have always and everywhere and of all been believed, within the Church of God.

But we are particularly concerned with the personal appropriation of Scripture in the life of prayer which will yield such treasure as is not superficially apparent. The treasure hid in a field, and the pearl of great price are the appropriate parables. [3] The treasure-house of Scripture is an abundant source of inspiration, a constant rule of life and a touchstone of faith.

Scripture is inseparably linked with prayer at different levels in the experience of the Christian. The person of prayer lives in the presence of God, constantly opening himself subjectively within his own heart, and objectively to the witness and teaching of Scripture. There are two basic ways in which Scripture feeds the life of prayer:

1 Praying with lectionary (reading with the Church)
2 Meditation in the secret place (devotional application).

Daily Lectionary Reading

The aspects of the life of prayer which are fed on Scripture must be grounded in discipline as well as charismatic freedom. Such discipline is displayed in reading with the Church. That means that there should be daily, disciplined and studied reading of Scripture in continuity. The life of prayer cannot be maintained on a selection of 'precious promises' from psalms, gospels and epistles arbitrarily chosen from a promise box. Devotional calendar paragraphs captioned by an out-of-context text from the corners of the minor prophets will not feed a hungry soul needing a staple diet.

Time, application and opportunity vary greatly. In my periods of solitude there was an abundance of Scripture read, chanted and sung in the long night office, at morning, midday and evening prayer and at Compline. The eucharistic passages were read even on days when the eucharist was not celebrated. Along with this was the detailed study of one of the readings from morning or evening prayer.

There are types of contemplative prayer in which the processes of discursive thinking are laid aside and the mind's activity is not encouraged, but in the daily offices and study, the sanctified mind is applied to the letter and spirit of Scripture. One studies context, content and contemporary application through a systematic approach to the written word.

The present ASB Church of England Lectionary contains three sets of readings for every day.[4] The eucharistic readings are the same as those of the Roman Catholic Church, and there are also psalms, Old Testament and New Testament lessons for morning and evening prayer. This lectionary may be purchased as a separate booklet annually, listing saints' days, themes and a lot of other invaluable information. There are also Scripture helps produced by Scripture Union or Bible Reading Fellowship readings with notes, and many other lectionary helps and aids. The point to be made is that the life of prayer needs the staple diet of daily, devotional reading of Scripture, preferably within a disciplined life of personal and corporate daily prayer, for by such a practice one is praying with the Church.

Prayer and the Psalms
Before considering the meditative reading of Scripture, special mention must be made of the psalter in prayer. Whatever other material one finds helpful in prayer, there is an objective *givenness* about Scripture and the psalter. Parts of the psalter reach back 3,000 years, into the spiritual history of vital religious experience, and we may be so bold as to say that not a day has passed when verses of the book of psalms have not been read, chanted or sung to the praise and worship of God.

Integral to the Life of Prayer
In the Christian tradition the psalms were taken over in unbroken succession from temple worship and Old Testament faith. Psalmody was part of Jesus' liturgical life and of the life of the early Church.[5] Psalms were used from earliest times not only in liturgical prayer, but in periods of great joy and sorrow. The discipline and spontaneity of marked hours of prayer in the life of the early disciples is evident in the story of Peter and John going to the temple to pray, and being open and charismatic enough to call upon the name of Jesus for the healing of the lame man at the Beautiful Gate.[6] In the story of Paul and Silas, beaten and fettered in prison for the sake of Christ at Philippi, we read that '. . . about midnight Paul and Silas were praying and singing hymns to God and the prisoners were listening to them, and suddenly there was a great earthquake, so that the foundations of the prison were shaken.'[7] One cannot help but believe that they were singing the forty-sixth psalm:

God is our refuge and strength:
a very present help in trouble.
Therefore we will not fear though the earth be moved:
and though the mountains are shaken in the midst of the sea.

That psalm indicates a great truth about the whole psalter. There is a revelation of objective truth about the nature and character of God and man, and yet there is a subjective appreciation and entering into transforming religious experience. The tumult of the world of nature and men does not terrify the man of prayer, for the psalm speaks in the depths of his heart: 'Be still and know that I am God.'

Microcosm of Human Frailty and Glory

There is a wrestling in prayer with the psalter, and in my own experience I have found it an agonizing experience to enter into a real appropriation of its power and relevance. It reflects both the glory of what it means to be human and the misery and helplessness of spiritual bankruptcy when one realizes one's own inadequacy, sinfulness and loneliness in the presence of the God who searches and knows all.[8]

There are psalms for joy and psalms for pain; psalms for praise and psalms for complaint. Some are so ecstatic that an earthly temple orchestra joins with the music of creation in jubilation. Some are so bitter that there is nothing but darkness and pain, and a descent into the dark underworld. There are variations of mood and climate; psalms for dancing and psalms for sackcloth and ashes. The psalter is a microcosm, a world in miniature, of the best and the worst of man's nature and estate.

The Imprecatory Psalms[9]

We could wax eloquent concerning the psalms of worship, adoration, beauty and splendour. They stand in the forefront of ancient inspired literature. But what do we say of the psalms of revenge, hatred, jealousy and spite?

It is not possible to gloss over such psalms. They have been a thorn in my flesh especially since I have been drawn into a deeper life of prayer and have found the psalter integral to such a life. The psalms in question have been called 'imprecatory' psalms, which bears the meaning of calling down vengeance upon one's enemies, especially in the form of cursing.

Christendom has always been perplexed as to what to do about them. Among the solutions are the following:

a. Admit, affirm, and carry out by force of arms the sentence spoken against the 'enemies of God'!
b. Omit the offending section;
c. Spiritualize the meaning, and turn it against spiritual evil and dark powers which militate against the divine Love;
d. Internalize the imprecations and curses against one's own sinfulness and apostasy.

The trouble is that many of these passages of vengeful imprecation are set in the midst of poems of such spiritual and literary beauty that one has to jump over the sections if one is omitting them, and busily reinterpret if one is including them. My own practice in community is to follow the custom of the friary, but in solitude, I recite the whole psalter, amending the imprecatory passages in the light of the reconciling gospel of Christ.

This sounds a somewhat arbitrary, risky and subjective practice, and there are particular problems of canonicity and authority involved which we have neither time nor space to discuss, but briefly I would state the matter thus:

a. The Mosaic ethical code stood for 'fracture for fracture, eye for eye, tooth for tooth'.[10] This was an improvement upon the surrounding heathen practice of a life for an eye and a life for a tooth.
b. Jesus was in continuity with the Mosaic tradition but superseded it by affirming a doctrine and practice of reconciliation. The whole of the fifth chapter of Matthew's gospel is taken up with: 'You have heard it said . . . but I say to you . . .' Part of the teaching runs:
   You have heard that it was said, 'An eye for an eye and a tooth for a tooth.' But I say to you, Do not resist one who is evil. But if anyone strikes you on the right cheek, turn to him the other also; . . .

You have heard that it was said, 'You shall love your neighbour and hate your enemy.' But I say to you, Love your enemies and pray for those who persecute you, so that you may be sons of your Father who is in heaven; for he makes his sun rise on the evil and the good, and sends rain on the just and on the unjust.[11]

c. So with the psalter. There is continuity in prayer and worship, but a gospel understanding of forgiveness and reconciliation, turning the curses into blessings, without ignoring the sinfulness and frailty of mortal man.

We do not explain away the cursings, neither do we condone them, or because it is the Bible, use them to justify our own petty hatreds and passions. But we must recognize that there is a certain release in expressing our worst passions and hatreds instead of repressing them. There are no social conventions which stop the ancient Hebrew from expressing himself completely – and it is refreshing to find such lack of constraint in prayer. We are perhaps overly sensitive in these areas, but we must remember that those were days of massacre, violence and blood sacrifices. It may be questioned whether we live in a more enlightened age, for as C. S. Lewis comments: 'We are, after all, blood-brothers to these ferocious, self-pitying barbaric men.'

In using these psalms as they are, and transposing them in the light of the Gospel (both of which I do), I realize again that there are perpetrators of injustice and oppression who deserve judgment, and there is such a thing as heinous sin. I realize also that all the evil, malice, darkness and cruelty spoken and complained of in the psalter is in my own soul. But more than all, I realize that the holy and judging God of the psalter is seen more truly and clearly in the light of the Gospel. He is not only a God of loving holiness, but supremely a God of holy love. And the Psalter is integral to a personal and corporate life of prayer and worship.

Saying, Singing and Chanting

These ancient psalm-poems become contemporary in their use – said, sung, or chanted. The Psalmist in exile becomes Paul and Silas in prison, Polycarp going to the stake, John of the Cross in his cell, Bunyan in Bedford gaol, Richard Wurmbrand in a communist prison, Bonhoeffer awaiting death in Flossenberg. They all found the psalter to be an immediate, contemporary and existential collection which enabled them to weep and laugh, to trust and complain, to cry out of the depths of loneliness and darkness to the one who knows all, sustains all, is everywhere present, and to whom darkness and light are both alike.[12]

The contemplative orders of men and women include a night office in their liturgical life, composed mostly of psalmody, either rising at night especially for the office, or beginning their day at 2.00 am or a little later. I felt the need for such an office, and rose early during my two long periods of solitude, and proved the value of saying or singing the psalter during the dark hours and alone. Exposure to the psalter at such depth taught me more of its meaning than I had learned in years of theological study and liturgical practice previously. There is no doubt that the psalter has sung and chanted itself into my very soul, and its inspiration is no mechanical or authoritative matter, but an experience of confrontation in which I have lived in praise and complaint, in joy and sorrow, in loneliness and ecstasy before and within the living God.

If spontaneity and discipline are inseparably part of our ongoing experience of prayer, we must find a disciplined and ordered method of using the psalter. This is already catered for in corporate liturgical worship, but we also need a method for private and personal prayer. The lectionary provides the appropriate daily psalms, and there are various ways of using them according to our musical and liturgical ability and taste. We may recite them audibly or mentally; we may monotone them on the one note; we may sing/chant them according to Anglican chant, Scottish metrical version or the ancient eight tones of plainchant which is my preferred method. There are other modern and simple methods such as the Gregory Murray tones or the popular Gelineau settings used by the brothers of Taize. Experiment until you find your own way, and consult those who are themselves experimenting with different forms and settings.

All we have said about the psalter must now be fitted into the context of our whole life of prayer. When we are praying the psalter, we are praying with the Church, but now we must consider the use of Scripture in its personal and meditative aspect.

Meditative Reading of Scripture

Meditation on Scripture may take various forms. It is differentiated from the formal, liturgical reading of Scripture in corporate times of prayer by the way in which a particular passage, verse or word is held in the mind and heart before God in a meditative manner. Reading moves into meditation and meditation into a contemplative feeding upon Scripture. Lectionary readings can, of course, be the basis of such meditation.

Supposing you take a scene from the life of Jesus. You allow yourself to be drawn into participation in the incident, and it becomes contemporary. You may feel the darkness and confusion of the man born blind, the uncleanness and rejection of the woman with the internal haemorrhage, or the sneering contempt of the common people for the tax-collector, Zacchaeus.[13] As the story unfolds you are drawn into an exposure to the divine Love, into the burning, searing and penetrating gaze of Jesus, into forgiveness, healing and reconciliation, in the company of the characters in the story.

Let me illustrate this by a simple incident that happened on the Maundy Thursday during my first Dorset period of solitude. Holy Week leads up to Easter, and the last three days – Maundy Thursday, Good Friday and Holy Saturday – move directly into the glory of Easter day. I had entered, more deeply than ever before, into the sadness and expectancy of Calvary and the hope of risen life.

Just before 4.00 am on Maundy Thursday morning I was awakened, and felt myself drawn out into the wooded area around the hut. I wrapped a blanket around me and stepped out into the darkness, but it was not entirely dark. There was a full moon and a covering of glistening frost upon the trees and ground, and I entered into Gethsemane. I had not engineered this or even prepared myself by the relaxing posture and breathing exercises which I practice before meditation. It was just that I was taken and led into the experience of Scripture. I moved toward a clump of trees and immediately was aware of being with Peter, James and John in Gethsemane. I looked at a clearing about thirty feet away, but I stood where I was, heavy in heart with the three disciples and yet touched with the wonder of the moment. There, in the clearing the Saviour was stretched on the ground, in agony and pleading. All around me was still, and there seemed to be a gulf fixed – I could not pass over. I had not learned the lesson of Gethsemane, but felt the sleepy helplessness of the disciples, unable to enter the loneliness and pain of Jesus. I could hear his words: 'Could you not watch with me one hour? – the spirit truly is willing, but the flesh is weak.'[14]

Then I stood quietly, wondering, in the silence of the early morning, and quietly began to sing:

> Lest I forget Gethsemane,
> Lest I forget your agony,
> Lest I forget your love for me,
> Lead me to Calvary.

I went back into the hut, said the night office and observed the period of silence. At about 5.15 am I went out again, and everything was different. Clouds covered the moon, it was darker and colder, and that brief period before dawn had lost the earlier beauty. I realized that I had been drawn into a Gethsemane experience which was already precious and heavy with secret meaning.

At 4.00 am the next morning, which was Good Friday,

I went out again. It seemed much colder, but the moon again was full, the frost glistening, but this time I was filled with overflowing gratitude, with such longing in my heart to really enter into the wonder of Calvary-love. The tune 'Bangor' played itself over in my mind, and I began to sing:

> Gethsemane can I forget?
> Or there thy conflict see,
> Thine agony and bloody sweat,
> And not remember thee?

and the rest of that hymn which has often caused me to enter into such prayer that I have had to remain at the foot of the cross, unable to go on with ordinary tasks for a while. After recording that experience in my journal, I added: 'And here alone, I can linger over such times with tears and distress at my coldness of heart and inability to love.'

These experiences were not geographical or historical journeys, but a contemplative and meditative form of praying Scripture. I did not see with my eyes the characters nor hear the words with my ears, but truly entered the situation in natural surroundings lit up by contemplative meditation. Sometimes, one is just 'visited' with such an experience. You may allow yourself to be gently led or powerfully driven by the Holy Spirit. More frequently it is a matter of making yourself open and available to God and Scripture. You yield yourself to God and He gives Himself to you, though the initiative is always with Him. Sometimes we may experience this directly as in the illustrations above, but even when we prepare ourselves by simple quietening of the body and mind we should understand that this, too, is a work of the Holy Spirit. We are made for prayer, for contemplative listening, and when the obstacles are removed, we are drawn deeper into God.

It is a good thing to have a spiritual reserve of Scripture within the heart for times of temptation and as a prerequisite for praying Scripture in the way we have described. There are certain basic passages which are packed full of spiritual and psychological truth and will reward a receptive and prayerful perusal after an initial period of centring and settling down. Take some of the following:

1 An account of the creation: Gen. 1:1–2:4;
2 The creation and fall of man: Gen. 2:5–3:4;
3 The Tower of Babel: Gen. 11:1–9;
4 Jacob's dream: Gen. 28:10–22;
5 Wrestling Jacob: Gen. 32:23–32;
6 The Joseph cycle: Gen. chapters 37 to 50;
7 The birth of Moses: Exod. 1:1–2:10;
8 The burning bush and mission of Moses: Exod. 3:1–15;
9 The glory of God on Sinai: Exod. 19:9–25;
10 The story of Ruth
11 Hannah's pilgrimage and prayer: 1 Sam. 1:1–28;
12 The boy Samuel: 1 Sam. 3:1–21;
13 David and Jonathan: 1 Sam. 18:1–5; 2O:1–21;
14 David's sin and repentance: 2 Sam. 12:1–15;
15 Solomon's dream and wisdom: 1 Kings 3:4–28;
16 The Elijah cycle: 1 Kings 17:1–21:29;
17 The Elisha cycle: 2 Kings chapters 2–8;
18 The story of Esther
19 The Song of Solomon
20 Chapters from the Evangelical Prophet: Isaiah 6:1–9 (prophetic call); 9:1–7 and 11:1–9 (messianic promises); 52:13–53:12 (suffering servant);
21 The valley of dry bones: Ezekiel 37:1–14;
22 The River of God: Ezekiel 47:1–12.

The wisdom literature of the Old Testament contains hidden treasures for meditative reading, and the above list provides a selection of appropriate passages for praying Scripture. As a child I learned a trite but memorable injunction about learning Scripture: 'Look it up/read it through/pray it in/live it out!' The first two are easier than the last two.

As to the New Testament, it is a simple matter to get hold of a Bible with a list of parables and miracles of Christ, or a harmony of the four gospels and work out a meditative plan from that. Alternatively, many of the new translations provide broken-up sections with captions and cross references. It is always worthwhile to consult the cross references.

I have before me a very good reference edition of *The Revised Standard Version* which contains all these helps, together with a consecutive daily reading plan covering the whole Bible in one year. But in terms of consecutive reading I still think the ASB lectionary with its abundant scriptural provision is the best available as long as one does not attempt too much and get discouraged.

Jesus Christ, the Living Word of God

There is an intimate connection between the life of prayer and the Word of God in Scripture. Scripture is the record, the witness of the breaking through of God's word into the experience of His prophets and people. The word of God as letter became incarnate in the prophetic ministry, and 'thus says the LORD' became the proclamation of the will of God to the world of men.

If the Word as letter and proclamation was so powerful an experience in the spiritual life of the Old Testament, how much more powerful when God himself becomes incarnate in the person of Jesus. This is not a question of a difference of degree, but of kind. The incarnation of the eternal Logos (Word) in Jesus is the visible manifestation of the eternal God. The praying Christian does not have to know all this consciously, but it is the theological basis of Christian mystical and contemplative prayer. The life of prayer, in the light of the incarnation of God in Jesus means not only that believers are in living communion and relationship with God in Jesus, but also that they are drawn into mystical union with God by the Holy Spirit – that prayer is the experience of the indwelling God in the hearts of his people.

It is not just that we *imitate* the loving compassion and

simple lifestyle of the human Jesus, but that we are *indwelt* by the crucified and risen Christ. The eternal Word-made-flesh did not only 'pitch his tent' in the midst of his human creation, but comes now to bring the glory of the eternal Father to indwell every receptive heart by the power of the Holy Spirit. We are drawn into the eternal circle of the Holy Trinity, indwelt by the living God, divinized by participation in His very life, made partakers of the divine nature.[15]

This is the fruition of God's will in the life of every person, but it is not fully understood except by those who open their body, mind and spirit to the entry of the divine Word. There is a sense in which the Word (Logos) already dwells in us, and at the heart of creation, for 'this is the true light that lightens every man that comes into the world', and 'in Him we live and move and have our being'. But there is a moment or a process, a cataclysmic encounter or an unfolding realization, when the living Word arises in the depths of our being – and prayer is born.

There is therefore a threefold sense in which the Word of God encounters the Christian in the life of prayer:

a. as the prophetic word of Scripture in the Old and New Testaments;
b. as the immanent Word or Logos at the heart of the created order;
c. as the Word incarnate in the person of our Lord Jesus Christ.

In other words – in prophecy, in creation and in redemption. If that is so then we will dwell in Him and He dwells in us. We shall encounter Him interiorly, in the written word of Scripture, and in all the deep places of creativity, joy and sorrow in our lives. Supremely, we shall experience him in the redeeming love of God in Jesus Christ, and to this there is no end, but an eternal unfolding.

References

1 James 5:16–18; 1 Thess. 5:16; Luke 11:5–13
2 2 Pet. 1:20
3 Matt. 13:44f.
4 Separate lectionary published annually, extracted from *The Alternative Service Book 1980*, London: SPCK.
5 Matt. 26:30; Mark 14:26; Eph. 5:19; Col. 3:16; James 5:13
6 Acts 3:1-10
7 Acts 16:25,26
8 Cf. pss. 8,73 and 88
9 Some 'imprecatory' elements are found in the following psalms: 58 *passim*; 68.21–23; 69:24–30; 83:9–18; 109:5–19; 137:7–9; 139:19–22; 140:9–11.
10 Exod. 21:24; Lev. 24:20; Deut. 19:21
11 Matt. 5:38,39,44,45
12 Ps. 139 *passim*.
13 John 9; Mark 10: 46–52; Mark 5: 24–34; Luke 19:1–10
14 Matt. 26:40,41
15 John 1:14; 2 Pet 1:4

7: The Jesus Prayer

Lord Jesus Christ, Son of God, have mercy on me, a sinner

Two Pictures

It is a Friday evening at the Anglican Chaplaincy of one of our Scottish Universities. The eucharist has been celebrated, and the mixed group of students and friends have shared fellowship and banter over a light supper. Now they are seated or kneeling in a semi-circle in the dimly-lit room-chapel. There is a period of quiet and 'settling down', a strong group awareness and an openness to a sense of the presence of God.

Quietly, one of the students, counting upon a simple string of 100 beads, begins to recite quietly and rhythmically what has come to be known as the Jesus Prayer: 'Lord Jesus Christ, Son of God, have mercy on me, a sinner.' The group gently takes up the prayer and recites it with him, some dropping out into silence, and others taking it up while he maintains the prayer and rhythm.

Then after fifty recitations, one of the girls takes the lead from him, and she is responsible for the next fifty recitations, while in the group some drop out, others join in, while some continue right through the 100 repetitions. The oral praying of the Jesus Prayer ends with the Gloria, and there is a continuing silence making up the half-hour or the hour which has been agreed beforehand.

The Chaplain, or one of the students, then leads the group in the saying or singing of the late night Office of Compline, after which the group breaks up in silence and leaves for home.

A second picture. The early morning service of Matins

has just ended at one of our friaries. One of the brothers has gone to the kitchen to prepare breakfasts for the friary family, while most of the remaining brothers settle down sitting, kneeling on their prayer-stools or cross-legged in the chapel for the morning meditation in silence. Very quietly, if one is near enough, one or more of the brothers could be observed going through a simple pattern of posture, relaxation and breathing, settling into a rhythmic movement of the Jesus Prayer on the outward and inward breaths or according to the rhythm of the heartbeat.

In these two pictures is illustrated a corporate and personal adaptation of the ancient Prayer of Jesus which originated in the Christian East among the Desert Fathers of the 3rd and 4th centuries, and is based biblically and theologically in the Christian tradition.

Biblical Basis

The substance of the Jesus Prayer is both a petition to the divine compassion and an adoration of the divine love. It is a prayer which has to be understood in the context of a firm trinitarian theology, recognizing that all prayer is inspired by the Holy Spirit, and directed to the glory of the Father, through the redemptive mediation of the Son, the Lord Jesus Christ.

The particular passages of Scripture which are immediately brought to mind by these words are found in the eighteenth chapter of Luke's Gospel. The first is the parable of the Pharisee and the Publican:[1]

He told this parable to some who trusted in themselves that they were righteous and despised others: 'Two men went up into the temple to pray, one a Pharisee and the other a tax collector. The Pharisee stood and prayed thus with himself, "God, I thank thee that I am not like other men, extortioners, unjust, adulterers, or even like this tax collector. I fast twice a week, I give tithes of all that I get." But the tax collector, standing far off, would not even lift up his eyes to heaven, but beat his breast, saying, "God be

119

merciful to me a sinner!'' I tell you, this man went down to his house justified rather than the other; for every one who exalts himself will be humbled, and he who humbles himself will be exalted.'

In one simple story, our Lord expounds the living dynamic of the Gospel of reconciliation, of full and free forgiveness to sinners, and of the justification of the unworthy sinner by the overflowing bounty of divine grace. Repentance and forgiveness are the key words beween man and God in this beautiful parable where human righteousness and pharisaism are shown up for the cheap and tawdry things they are, and the truly sorrowful heart is made new.

The second passage occurs later in the chapter, and is the account of the healing of the blind man at Jericho:[2]

As he drew near to Jericho, a blind man was sitting by the roadside begging; and hearing a multitude going by, he inquired what this meant. They told him, 'Jesus of Nazareth is passing by.' And he cried, 'Jesus, Son of David, have mercy on me!' And those who were in front rebuked him, telling him to be silent; but he cried out all the more, 'Son of David, have mercy on me!' And Jesus stopped, and commanded him to be brought to him; and when he came near, he asked him, 'What do you want me to do for you?' He said, 'Lord, let me receive my sight.' And Jesus said to him, 'Receive your sight; your faith has made you well.' And immediately he received his sight and followed him, glorifying God; and all the people, when they saw it, gave praise to God.

Evangelical Conversion
When I first located this passage indicated by the Jesus Prayer, I recalled a gospel song which was inspired by this miracle-story and which was true to my own evangelical experience of the Gospel:

One sat alone beside a highway begging,
His eyes were blind, the light he could not see;
He clutched his rags, and shivered in the shadows,
Then Jesus came – and bade the darkness flee.

When Jesus comes, the tempter's power is broken!
When Jesus comes, the tears are wiped away!
He takes the gloom, and fills the life with glory,
For all is changed, when Jesus comes to stay.

The element of persistence and repetition is emphasized in this story, and the constantly repeated words reveal the determination and seriousness in the blind petitioner that calls attention both to his utter need and to his awareness of the person of Jesus:

Jesus, Son of David, have mercy on me!
Jesus, Son of David, have mercy on me!
Jesus, Son of David, have mercy on me!

It is impossible not to hear the constant repetition of the liturgical words of the beginning of the ancient eucharistic rites, chanted, sung and shouted through the ages in all parts of the Church:

Kyrie eleison!   Lord, have mercy!
Christe eleison!   Christ, have mercy!
Kyrie eleison!   Lord, have mercy!

The post-biblical origins of the Jesus Prayer are found in the deserts of Palestine, Egypt and Syria, where the Desert Fathers lived lives of simplicity and prayer as a positive vocation to God's glory, and as a witness against the worldliness of the Constantinian Church which was increasingly accommodating itself to the world. Apart from the abundant literature on the development of the Prayer in the Christian East,[3] we are in the midst of a contemporary revival of interest and practice of the Prayer in both East and West.

A simple 'technique' has evolved which is effective in the use of this Prayer, but is not essential to it. Some people find a technique extremely helpful, while others find it a distraction. The Jesus Prayer itself as a form, is one which, though it has increasing contemporary popularity and use, will not suit every Christian's temperament or ability. One does not have to come from the Orthodox tradition of the East to practice this Prayer with great spiritual profit. It can be taken up with great joy by those of a Western Catholic or Evangelical tradition. And the consequences may be a greater freedom and depth in prayer than ever known before. I discovered the repetition of the name of Jesus in adoration among the classic Pentecostals long before I found the Jesus Prayer in the Orthodox tradition!

Repetition

A word about repetition. We have been careful to ground the Jesus Prayer in Scripture, but one does not do that by the quotation of random verses to justify non-scriptural practices! Jesus said: 'And in praying do not heap up empty phrases (AV: vain repetitions) as the Gentiles do; for they think that they will be heard for their many words . . . your Father knows what you need before you ask him.'[4]

It is quite clear that Jesus is inveighing against another form of pharisaism – that of the vain multiplication of words to be repeated in the sight of men, or as a work of merit to be set in the columns of some divine ledger, which was the basis of pharisaic religion. The Jesus Prayer acknowledges the divine mercy, the free grace of God, by which alone salvation is to be received. There is no place here for the legalistic works-salvation of the pharisee. The multiplication of religious words from an hypocritical heart finds no acceptance in the scheme of God's salvation. The whole weight of the Old Testament revelation at its highest informs the teaching of Jesus at this point, as Jesus quotes: 'Well did Isaiah prophesy of you, when he said: "This people honours me with their lips, but their heart is far from me, teaching as doctrines the precepts of men"'[5]

It is not repetition *per se*, but vain repetition, wordy multiplication, empty religiosity that our Lord is speaking against. But the repetition of repentance and adoration is of another order. The opening *Kyries* of the eucharist, together with the persistent words of the blind man of Jericho indicate the heartfelt cry from sinful and sorrowing humanity which calls down the divine compassion. It is the divine compassion which inspires these words in the first place, for we are unable to repent of ourselves.

The repetition of adoration is of a different category, but truly elevates and fulfils the cry of penitence, and shares in its personal and corporate nature. Let us take an Old Testament and then a New Testament example.

Repetition in Adoration

One of the classic chapters of prophetic call in the Old Testament is the sixth chapter of Isaiah's prophecy. Within the context of the heavenly worship the call, purification and commission of the prophet takes place. It is all in the nature of spiritual vision. On the one hand there is the revelation of the divine glory and holiness, and on the other Isaiah's mortality and sinfulness brings him to penitence and confession. As the picture is graphically described by the prophet[6] one can almost hear the incessant chanting of the seraphim calling antiphonally one to another:

> Holy, holy, holy is the Lord of hosts;
> The whole earth is full of his glory.

The vision is a door into heaven, a transient glimpse into the unending adoration ascribed to the LORD (Yahweh) in his threefold being and glory.

In the New Testament Apocalypse there is another picture of the heavenly court which John beheld 'in the

Spirit'[7]. John the Divine, like Ezekiel, is reticent to describe quite what he saw, for the central throne is filled with light and glory and is surrounded by an emerald rainbow. The whole people of God are symbolized by the twenty-four (2 × 12) elders clothed with righteousness and splendour, and the sevenfold Spirit of God manifests his luminous wisdom in thunder, lightning and the mysterious crystal sea. The four living creatures surrounding the throne reflect the divine glory, and lead the heavenly worship. They are winged like seraphim, bear the attributes of created being, and are full of intuitive knowledge:

> and day and night they never cease to sing,
> 'Holy, Holy, Holy, is the Lord God Almighty,
> who was and is and is to come'.

The response to such acclamation and adoration with incense and fire, is the worship offered by the twenty-four elders who prostrate themselves before the throne, crying:

> Worthy art thou, our Lord and God,
> to receive glory and honour and power,
> for thou didst create all things,
> and by thy will they existed and were created.

The high, dramatic moment is the appearance of the Lamb who has been slain from the foundation of the world, now risen and endued with the omniscience of the sevenfold Spirit. He becomes the centre of glory and adoration within the trinitarian revelation, and the song of creation becomes the song of redemption. Myriads upon myriads of adoring creatures representing all hierarchies and orders of being throughout the whole universe cry out, time and time again:

> 'Worthy is the Lamb who was slain to receive power
> and wealth and wisdom and might and honour and
> glory and blessing!' And I heard every creature in

heaven and on earth and under the earth and in the sea, and all therein, saying, 'To him who sits upon the throne and to the Lamb be blessing and honour and glory and might for ever and ever!' And the four living creatures said, 'Amen!' and the elders fell down and worshipped.

The point we are making here is that in profound penitence and in adoring worship, there is a repetitive liturgical expression of pain and glory that participates in the wonder of God. It is initiated by the indwelling Spirit of God, and is both intensely personal and profoundly corporate in its expression. All orders of created and redeemed being are caught up into such glory, and it flows back to its source in the mystery of God the Father. This is the quality of penitence and adoration that is found in the simplicity and profundity of repetition in the Jesus Prayer.

The Stages of the Prayer
Before we speak of the practical aspects of the Jesus Prayer, we should note the important distinction which is made between the three degrees or stages at which the Prayer is experienced – the lips, the mind and the heart.

Much has been written concerning these stages, but there is a chapter in Abhishiktananda's book *Prayer*, entitled 'The Holy Name', where the matter is presented simply and concisely. Abhishiktananda was a French Benedictine monk who lived a life of exemplary simplicity and holiness in India for over 25 years and who died a few years ago in his beloved and adopted country. He was a man of prayer and theology, of mind and heart – a rare combination. He had a rare gift also, of personal and literary communication. I commend his book and summarize his exposition.

The first stage in the praying of the Jesus Prayer is to pray it audibly with the lips. The mind may be distracted or even full of carnal and irrelevant desires. Don't get anxious or worried about that, for the prayer will do its own work under the Holy Spirit. The important thing is that the believer should repeat the Name with reverence and a longing for the Lord.

In the second stage the lips are closed. The prayer continues in the mind, and there is a thoughtful attention to the Name. It is not an exercise in mental concentration; there is no striving to eject other thoughts, and no anxious mental effort, just a free simple awareness of the Prayer. If there are distractions, buzzing thoughts, what someone has called a monkey-tree mind, let them be, do not strain, but gently, simply, always return to the Prayer, return to the Prayer, return to the Prayer.

In the third stage the Prayer, or the Name, is placed in the heart. The lips and vocal chords are silent and the mind becomes quiet. The Prayer is lodged in the very centre of the being, the cave of the heart. There are many variations of this third stage, from beginners to those who have dwelt within the Name of Jesus for many years. The apprenticeship may take the whole of one's life, but within this third stage there are glimpses of complete, quiet resting in God. All desires are transformed, and pass into the sole desire for the Lord, to contemplate his glory, to enter more deeply into union with him. The great contemplatives who have practised the Jesus Prayer recommend that it be uttered (though inaudibly) according to the rhythm of the respiration or heartbeat. Thus the whole being – body, soul, sense and mind – are taken up into the Prayer, and the whole universe also, of which the body is a part.

In the Greek and Russian Orthodox tradition, at the clothing of a monk, he is given a prayer rope with a hundred knots, and is told by his Abbot that he must always have the Name of the Lord Jesus on his lips, in his mind and in his heart. By such a threefold distinction it is clear that the Jesus Prayer may be used quite simply by any believer who loves the Name of Jesus. Like the river that flowed from the throne in the book of Ezekiel,[9] the Jesus Prayer, flowing from the heart of God, may be waters in which to paddle, in which to wade, in which to swim, opening into the profound depths of the contemplative life. But everywhere the river flows it will bring fertility, life and freshness.

This means that although it is a prayer that can be used to express penitence, love and adoration, if the Prayer is used with deep desire for God, born of the Holy Spirit, then more time will be given and more depth attained; it will then become necessary to find someone who is experienced in the life of prayer generally, and especially in the Jesus Prayer, with whom one can share. The Jesus Prayer must not be isolated from the ongoing life of eucharist and worship in the Body of Christ, for depth in prayer will expose the Christian to areas of darkness within himself which cannot be faced alone. Some of these areas will be dealt with later.

Practice: Posture, Breathing and Heartbeat

As we think of actually beginning to practise the Jesus Prayer as one of the ways of entering more deeply into the love of God, let it be clear that this is but a method. It is a good method for many, one which I have found invaluable in my own experience, but it is merely a way of preparation and opening up to God. No method, no technique of prayer can bring about an awareness of God's presence automatically – God is sovereign and free and under no compulsion. Prayer is not magic and not manipulative! God's loving presence and the experience of His holiness is a gift of free and unmerited grace. But having said that, it is a simple, biblical and flexible method to use the Jesus Prayer, which brings body, mind and heart into the experiential awareness of God in Christ.

The first thing to do is to find a place of quiet where you will not be disturbed.[10] Then following the method we have described in our chapter on the body, choose a posture in which you can be relaxed and yet alert. You may find it appropriate to stand, sit, kneel, sit cross-legged, using a prayer-stool or cushion, or even to lie down on your tummy or back. It is always a good practice to keep the back straight. Then using some simple words of faith and affirmation, bring yourself into a unity of concentration, relaxing each part of your body, from the crown of your head, to the soles of your feet. Settle down gently in this relaxed position, and take note of the rate and rhythm of your breathing.

Let your breathing slow down and become deeper, breathing from your diaphragm rather than your chest (belly breathing not chest breathing).

Note the deep, slow inspiration, the slight pause, the expiration. Follow your breathing, giving attention to regularity with gentleness. Let nothing be forced, but more and more surrender your tensions to the inward work of the Holy Spirit. It is possible, after a few minutes of such relaxed breathing, to gently begin to repeat the prayer on the expiration and inspiration of the breath. But let us first take note of the heartbeat. There is no need to take one's pulse at the radial or other pulse-points, for if you have brought yourself into a posture of relaxation and your breathing is slow, deep and rhythmic, you will soon be able to feel your heartbeat. If you have not done this before it may take a little getting used to, and it may be a help to take your radial pulse, counting gently the beats (at rest between 70 and 80 beats a minute – this varies with individuals). When you are aware of the body pulse, and your whole body is pulsing with the heart, then let your mind focus upon the loveliness of Christ as Lord and Saviour, and begin quietly to repeat the words of the Jesus Prayer, according to the heartbeat:

1 Lord Jesus
2 Christ
3 Son
4 of God,

5 have mercy
6 on me,
7 a sinner.
8 *Pause*

You may find this too fast even for a slow, steady pulse, and certainly if you are participating in a group saying the Jesus Prayer, then the leader of the group will regulate the prayer at a slower rhythm. It is a matter of practice, and you will find that it is easier to keep the pulse rate with the prayer when it is said mentally.

But some people find themselves more at home with the Prayer in the outbreaths and inbreaths, remembering what we have said about the Holy Spirit as the Breath of God and the principle of both physical and spiritual life. You may proceed:

Exhalation:	Lord Jesus Christ,
Inhalation:	Son of God,
Exhalation:	have mercy on me,
Inhalation:	a sinner.

The respiration has already been slowed to a steady and rhythmic rate, and there should be no effort involved in the saying of the prayer. It will become clear how important posture, relaxation, and sparse, loose clothing is when one is using the heartbeat or breath to accompany the prayer. The use of a 100 knotted rope, or a string of 50 or 100 wooden beads with one large knot or bead to mark the end can be useful in a Jesus Prayer Group, or if one is using 100 or 200 repetitions to begin a time of silence. Otherwise, such an aid can be dispensed with, though there are many who use the rope not only for counting, but as a means of concentrating and stilling the mind as the fingers move from knot to knot.

Walking the Jesus Prayer
This is done in the country, a large park or by the sea, or in any private place where there are not many people or any traffic. The steps must be measured and slow and meditative, and the prayer may be verbal or mental, ultimately descending 'into the heart' as we have noted the stages of the Jesus Prayer.

Any time of day is suitable for this meditation, though early morning and late evening are good times for it. Before setting out on a walk it is good practice to adopt a meditation posture before the Lord for a few minutes, with a prayer of invocation for the Holy Spirit to guide one's steps and heart.

It is assumed that you are wearing something like a tracksuit or loose clothing, so after a few minutes start out on the walk, setting the pace in a slow, measured, rhythmic step according to the fourfold Jesus Prayer, thus:

1st step:	Lord Jesus Christ,
2nd step:	Son of God,
3rd step:	have mercy on me,
4th step:	a sinner.

It may take a minute or two to get into the measured tread that is suitable, and you may feel a bit foolish the first time, but as soon as it is established, the prayer on the lips can become the prayer in the mind. The way will then be open for the Lord to place it deep within the heart and it will begin to pray itself. This is another way of saying that the Holy Spirit will be praying the prayer in and through you, to the glory of God the Father.

There are no rules as to the period of time to be spent in this Jesus Prayer Walk. It may well be that you will walk for a half-hour, and then return in silence, allowing the Lord's presence to remain in the silence of the same measured pace.

Jesus on the lips, in the mind, in the heart
Now let us note the three stages we have mentioned above – the lips, the mind and the heart. The first stage seems clear – the audible praying of the prayer. It recalls the simplest beginnings of calling upon the Name of the Lord for salvation.[11] This is the stage at which many Christians stay for the whole of their lives – the stage of 'talking' and never waiting upon God. While one is speaking prayers the mind is engaged, and the problem of letting go into silence is that buzzing distractions and inappropriate thoughts and desires invade the mind. There is deep theological meaning in every word of the

130

Jesus Prayer, and there is a time for a theological and devotional appreciation of them, but the first stage of the Jesus Prayer is also the stage in which the mind is given something to do – a repetition of the words, and a constant returning to the words when distractions come. The words can then wash over the soul, and the deeper reaches of the mind can become occupied with the silence and receptivity in which God manifests Himself. Therefore it is counterproductive in the first stage to fight against wandering or invasive thoughts, for tension is involved in such conflict. It is wise to ignore them, be indifferent to them, don't embrace them or strive against them in your own strength, just continually return, return to the Prayer, over and over again.

The second stage is a letting go into the silence. There may have been some meditative movement of the mind in the first stage, in evaluating and appropriating the spiritual meaning of the Jesus Prayer. But now the mind takes over the repetition from the lips, and there is a quieting of the thinking processes. The analogy of being in love, of resting quietly in the beloved without involvement of the logical thinking processes illustrates this second stage. The believer remains in the simple, experiential awareness of Jesus. This can happen suddenly, or it may take place gradually, or one can go on for a long time before experiencing this simple resting in pure awareness. And there is always the possibility of lapsing back into logical thinking or being invaded again by the buzzing thoughts which come uninvited and have nothing to do with the matter in hand. Don't despair, don't give up, just return to the Prayer – again and again.

In the third stage the Name of Jesus is placed in the 'heart'. Using the word 'heart' we have the ancient Semitic and Old Testament usage in mind which indicates not only the emotions, but the deep, inward part of man – in a sense the totality of man's being. We have to make the inward journey to the centre of one's being where the Holy Spirit dwells and reigns in the life of the dedicated believer.

Because of the work of such men as Carl G. Jung, we have become aware of levels of being that go much further than conscious awareness. They may be thought of as interpenetrating layers which include the conscious, subliminal consciousness (thought of as the sub- or unconscious), and the collective unconscious. A Hebrew and Christian doctrine of man, followed especially by the Eastern Fathers, thinks of man as an impenetrable mystery, known only by the Spirit of God.[12] Pioneers in the field of psychology and psychiatry such as Freud, Jung and Adler have done a service to Christian and secular man in calling attention to dimensions of being in which biblical modes of thought may operate freely. Certainly, their findings may help us in an understanding of the deeper reaches of prayer.

This third stage of the Jesus Prayer, moves into a depth of resting in the loving awareness of God in Christ in which the action of God's Holy Spirit is primary. It is not that the believer prays the prayer, but that it is being prayed in and through him. The doctrine of mystical union with Christ in God is the very experience of the believer. The living fountain which Jesus promised is springing up in the believer's heart, and the promise he made on the Great Day of the Feast of Tabernacles is being fulfilled: 'He who believes in me, as the Scripture has said, "Out of his heart shall flow rivers of living water."'[13] And Jesus was speaking of the indwelling Spirit. The word which is rendered 'heart' in *The Revised Standard Version* is translated in many different ways in modern translations, endeavouring to communicate the idea of the innermost sanctuary of man's being.

The Way of a Pilgrim

As well as the teaching of the Fathers of the East and the monks of Mount Sinai and Mount Athos, and that unique compendium on the Jesus Prayer called *The Philokalia*, there is much contemporary writing on the subject. But at this point it would be timely to refer to *The Way of a Pilgrim*. This is the wonderful story of an anonymous

19th century Russian peasant who walked through days and nights throughout Russia seeking to know the fullness of meaning contained in St Paul's words: 'Pray without ceasing'[14] which he had heard at mass.

After much disappointed seeking he meets a *staretz* (elder or wise one) who instructs him in the way of the Jesus Prayer. His way is not easy, and his lifestyle is that of a wandering pilgrim. 'My worldly goods are a knapsack with some dried bread in it on my back,' he says, 'and in my breast pocket a Bible. And that is all.' He spends much time in the first and second stages of the prayer, with much difficulty and suffering as well as times of great joy and peace. Then, in a further pilgrimage to the tomb of St Innocent of Irkutsk in Siberia, the Lord visits him with the gift of The Prayer of Jesus:

> After no great lapse of time I had the feeling that the Prayer had, so to speak, by its own action passed from my lips to my heart. that is to say, it seemed as though my heart in its ordinary beating began to say the words of the Prayer within at each beat. Thus for example, *one*, 'Lord,' *two*, 'Jesus,' *three*, 'Christ,' and so on. I gave up saying the Prayer with my lips. I simply listened carefully to what my heart was saying. It seemed as though my eyes looked right down into it; and I dwelt upon the words of my departed staretz when he was telling me about this joy. Then I felt something like a slight pain in my heart, and in my thoughts so great a love for Jesus Christ that I pictured myself, if only I could see Him, throwing myself at His feet and not letting them go from my embrace, kissing them tenderly, and thanking Him with tears for having of His love and grace allowed me to find so great a consolation in His Name, me, His unworthy and sinful creature! Further there came into my heart a gracious warmth which spread through my whole breast.[15]

This little book has met a real need in the lives of many active Christians who are seeking a simple way into the profound mystery of God's love. We have said that the Jesus Prayer is personal yet not individualistic. It has a communal orientation, and the expectation is that the one who practises the prayer is a Christian steeped in the Scriptures, a member of the Body of Christ who receives holy communion as part of a regular sacramental life.

It would be well, therefore, before attempting this method of prayer, to find someone who is acquainted with it and share initial experience with him, or else find a group that already meets to say the Jesus Prayer, and then do some simple experimental exercises to see if this is the way for you. We conclude with words of a wise staretz, Theophan the Recluse,[16] who offers his advice:

> I will remind you of only one thing: one must descend with the mind into the heart, and there stand before the face of the Lord, ever present, all-seeing within you. The prayer takes a firm and steadfast hold, when a small fire begins to burn in the heart. Try not to quench this fire, and it will become established in such a way that the prayer repeats itself: and then you will have within you a small murmuring stream.

References

1 Luke 18: 9–14
2 Luke 18: 35–43
3 See G. E. H. Palmer (ed), *The Philokalia*, London: (Faber & Faber, 1979).
4 Matt. 6:7,8
5 Matt. 15:8,9; Cf. Micah. 6:6–8; Isa. 58:3–9
6 Isa. 6:1–8
7 Rev. 4:2
8 Rev. 5:11–14
9 Ezek. 47:1–9
10 Matth. 6:6

11 Rom. 10:9

12 1 Cor. 2:11

13 John 7:38

14 1 Thess. 5:17

15 R. M. French, (trans), *The Way of a Pilgrim*, p. 32. London: (SPCK 1930).

16 See also Theophan the Recluse (ed) *Unseen Warfare*, ch. 'On the Jesus Prayer', pp. 241 ff. London: (Mowbrays, 1978).

8: Time for God: Retreats and Hut Spirituality

Family Meditation

We have no time to pray. We are too busy! I have a friend who is a potter. He is married with two small children. His wife is Hindu and he is on a periphery of the Christian Church with a great reverence and love for the person of Jesus, though he would not be able to state an allegiance in doctrinal terms. Some time ago, after he had spent some time in prayerful retreat at the friary, I went home with him for a meal and a pottery lesson. I met his wife, four-year-old Emlyn, and the baby brother. 'Shall we have a time of meditation before throwing some pots?' Donald asked. I was happy to do this, and so while baby brother was asleep, Donald, his wife and Emlyn led the way to the meditation room upstairs in their little Dorset cottage. We all took our appropriate posture for prayer, and I noticed that little Emlyn sat in semi-lotus position, ready to sound the shrutti-box which is a kind of one-note concertina for chanting. We spent some time in quietness, and then Donald and his wife began a gentle, plaintive chant, and quietness again. After some more silence, I began to sing:

> Jesus, how lovely you are,
> You are so gentle, so pure and kind;
> You shine like the morning star,
> Jesus, how lovely you are.

and they all joined me.

I didn't notice a television set in the cottage, the lifestyle was simple, the food vegetarian and wholesome.

They are a well-educated but unsophisticated young married couple who find it financially difficult at times. But they have time to pray.

I am not making any doctrinal evaluation of their religious standing, nor am I writing these paragraphs as an ecumenical exercise. I am concerned to point out that Donald and his little family have meditation and prayer at the heart of their life. When we left the meditation room and went into the pottery, Donald demonstrated 'throwing a pot', and I had my first try. It succeeded, and he said, 'Ramon, you threw the clay and got it centred nicely, I think it shows that you are centred within yourself.' I'm afraid that was probably more encouragement than truth, but it did set me thinking about being 'centred' in myself by prayer, meditation and love. I was reminded of God as the heavenly potter and of ourselves as malleable clay. I went in heart with Jeremiah to the potter's house,[1] and marvelled with him at the wonderful patience of the Lord in taking again the marred vessel and remaking it, and I began to sing quietly in my heart:

Have your own way, Lord, have your own way,
You are the potter, I am the clay;
Mould me and make me after your will,
As I am waiting, yielded and still.

Make time to pray
The point I am making is clear. We need time to pray, and most of us can make time to pray. I know there are some people whose lives are so full of family responsibilities that it seems impossible to get time. Well do I remember the grateful mothers who left their toddlers at playschool in the church hall of my Upper Norwood Parish! And when such mothers (and fathers) get some free time, they are often too exhausted or anxious to be able to pray.

I want to address part of this chapter to people like that, but also to the majority of Christian people who profess to have no time, but whose lives are cluttered with unnecessary work, unprofitable television, meetings, committees, entertainments and time-wasting occupations which are holding them back from the primary thing for which they were made – communion with God. It is also addressed to Christians who are lazy and slothful, or who are frenetic and workaholic.

'You have made us for yourself,' says Augustine before God, 'and our hearts are restless until they rest in you.' The contemplative vision of creation and redemption is one in which we find ourselves actually participating with the forgiving, reconciling, sustaining and creative God. If we do not live out this communion with God from the depth of our being, our lives will become dissatisfied, unproductive and lacking in the very qualities which are most human – namely, compassion and love.

Obviously, if you are going to put into practice even part of the commended practices included in this book you will need time. It is true that I have had two six-month periods of complete solitude, and freedom to explore the paths of prayer about which I write. But I had to stop in my frenetic and busy life and take stock of who I was and where I was going. I had to call a halt, reorientate myself, seek God in prayer and do His will. They were not easy decisions, but I cannot go back on them.

There are times in the lives of our brothers and sisters when they are so overwhelmed by the pressure of the human need to which they minister that there seems no time for personal prayer and meditation apart from the liturgical offices. We have a school for emotionally maladjusted boys; St Francis' Home, where we care for a dozen or so men, a house which takes in people who need pastoral care for months at a time after domestic, sexual or financial crisis, and we have houses for young people on probation, work with wayfarers, work among multiracial groups and involvement in educational and social work. This is quite apart from our guesthouses where we minister to individual and group spiritual and pastoral needs, and the evangelistic and ministry missions which are going on continually. All this calls for deep commitment, untiring energy and physical resources which seem more than we can command. That is why we need time for prayer. Listen to part of our rule:

> The brothers and sisters must strive ever to remember how essential is the work of prayer to every department of their lives. Without the constant renewal of divine grace the spirit flags, the will is weakened, the conscience grows dull, the mind loses its freshness and even the bodily vigour is impaired. They must, therefore, always be on their guard against the constant temptation to let other work encroach upon the hours of prayer, remembering that if they seek in this way to increase the bulk of their activity, it can only be at the cost of its true quality and value.[2]

Plan a Time

It is no use waiting to see if you have time. It is not fair to give to God the bits of spare time in which you are too tired or confused or tense to pray. You must draw up a plan: see the need as primary, find a place that is private, unload your responsibilities for that time on a member of the family, a neighbour, a friend.

It is impossible for me to be specific because I do not know your situation. If you have children to care for you will have to think of playschool, nursery, or a baby-sitter. People pay a sitter for a 'night out', why not for prayer? If you have a job which begins at 8.00 am or later, you must get up earlier (therefore go to bed earlier!). If you start work before 7.00 am, then after work and before evening is your time. If your work necessitates a bath or shower, then let that be the beginning of your meditation. Perhaps you can give up the car and bus, and either cycle or jog to work. If you are on shift work, then make meditation-time a part of your planning. One reads continually of sporting celebrities who take their play joyfully and seriously allowing time for relaxation-meditation immediately before their professional activity – it pays dividends.

Start with an hour a day, divided into reading and meditation at first. A little time every day is better than a chunk on Sundays! If you are in love you surely have time to think about, write to, or meet your lover every day. Otherwise I wonder if you are in love!

When you have established the discipline of an hour a day, then give to the Lord part of a day, then a day in a week, then two days in a month. And that brings me to a week in a year – a retreat!

Retreat

The word may sound a bit negative, but it is not primarily a retreat *from* the world, though it is also that. It is rather a retreat *into* God, into silence, into love. I would say that the best kind of retreat is one which is useless, where you learn nothing. Have you misunderstood me? To be utilitarian, constantly productive, ever-learning, compelled by a work ethic which makes money, saves time, increases goods, is the bane of our Western life. To make a week's retreat in which you let go completely and let the Holy Spirit move freely within and around you could be the watershed of your life. Of course there are varieties of retreats. Think about the following:

1 A corporate, conducted retreat which includes fellowship, ministry, pastoral care, soul-friend sharing, daily eucharist and offices.
2 A conducted retreat in silence, apart from a daily meeting with the retreat conductor for an hour each morning when he/she gives you Scripture and there is a minimum of sharing. Daily eucharist may be included.
3 An unconducted retreat in silence with some reading input, or none save for Scripture. This could be in a hut or hermitage attached to a friary or monastery.
4 A corporate, thematic retreat, e.g. on healing, meditation, lifestyle or gospel-compassion. This may incorporate practical instruction and sharing in laying-on-of-hands, fasting, etc.

Experimentation is a key-word here, for we are all different. In the same hermit vocation there are hardly two hermits who follow the same pattern. Some are 'idiorhythmic' which may be translated 'doing your own thing'. It is good to have some manual work and physical exercise for part of the day, and necessary to work out diet, fasting periods, and give forethought to personal needs. The retreat in the context of a friary, monastery or retreat house ensures that domestic matters are taken care of, but a bit of planning is needed for the first time in a hermitage. A first-time silent retreat will anyway need a responsible person available – just in case! Strange things happen in silence!

Spiritual director, Soul-friend, Conductor

If you are not familiar with terms like spiritual director, soul friend, retreat conductor, these are categories which have evolved in the pastoral ministry of the Church, and such persons presumably have certain spiritual gifts of ministry, discernment, spiritual direction and speak primarily from spiritual experience in theology and prayer. They may be men or women, ordained or lay, and they manifest the ministry-gifts within the Body of Christ, and bear charisms of the Holy Spirit.[3]

The Christian who has such a director/soul-friend is indeed fortunate, for participation in the deeper reaches of prayer makes such an experienced person necessary. The ministry of sharing and penitence in the early Church was a spiritual mutuality within a network of apostolic love and gentle authority.[4]

Chronos and Kairos

Paul Tillich makes much of the New Testament distinction between the two words for time, *chronos* which is clock time, and *kairos* which is the moment of decision, maturity and readiness.[5] (Contrast Matthew 2:7, *chronos* with Matthew 21:34, *kairos*). Within the time-flow of quantitative time, God calls us to qualitative times of decision, of renewal, of confrontation, of prayer, leading to deeper union with Himself. These are God's moments, and when they occur we must be ready. Time for God is a prime necessity and a priority in our lives.

Jesus was aware that His coming was in fulfilment of the divine *kairos*, and He felt His time, His hour of passion and glory drawing near.[6] So there are moments of *kairos* in our lives when discovery, enlightenment and challenge confront and invade us. Time is a precious commodity in our world. 'I haven't got time – I'm too busy' is heard on every hand, and there is no time to 'waste'. But if you are too busy for God, then you are just too busy! I've never met anyone who possesses a TV set who had no time to view! We need to waste time with God as we would waste time on a loved one – not doing or planning or thinking, but simply *being* in His presence and resting in His love. We cannot dictate to God the time or manner of His revelation to us, for He is free and sovereign, and His *kairos* is dependent upon His own loving will. Yet he calls upon us to wait on Him, to gaze upon His glory, to spend time prodigiously, so that we are open and receptive to the *kairos* of his revelation to us.[7]

Hut Spirituality

Let me return to the 'two days a month' idea. One of the things I have suggested to groups and families who are looking for time to pray is the communal purchase of a hut – a garden shed, about 12′ × 10′ or larger. I lived in a 12′ × 6′ hut for six months and found it a little cramped sometimes. One of the group may have a sizeable garden or access to such a place, and the financial purchase and equipping of it would be shared. Basic needs would be a divan bed (could be a door on breeze-blocks with mattress); a portable camping-gas burner (two rings and a grill) with two cylinders; access to water (a butt), and a portable outside toilet (Elsan). Domestic needs (crockery, shelves, etc) can be catered for by mutual planning, but basic needs would also include a table, chair and source of light. It is advisable for the hut to be lined within and creosoted without. Such a hut provides a place of solitude and silence on the pattern of the old desert fathers and Celtic monks who lived in wooden, wattle and rough-hewn dwellings, and if one wanted ancient authority for such a hut spirituality there is precedent in the schools of the prophets under Elijah and Elisha.[8]

In my hut I had an icon of the Pantokrator (Christ the Almighty) on the wall, and a small altar-table with Rublev's icon of the Holy Trinity, a burning light and a Bible always open at the gospel of the day and a prayer-stool. Carpeting is a luxury but so good on winter mornings!

It is exciting to plan such a venture, especially if a vegetable garden is included. But the important thing is that it is a place of silence and of prayer. It is *not*, repeat *not*, a holiday hut. Once you let it be used as such, that is the end of prayer. This does not mean that one does not sleep in recuperation and recreation, but once the primary significance is compromised, other ideas, equipment and needs take over.

With this basic place, the group can draw up a time-table so that members may have at least a whole day (two nights) in solitude with the Lord. Your local priest or pastor may share in the dedication of the hut to the Lord, and there may be a simple group service of claiming the ground for the Lord in a Jericho procession with a dedication eucharist. But the less fuss the better, for it is not meant to be advertised outside the group, but to be hidden. People are *not* to visit it socially outside their allotted time.

The hidden aspect of such a hut becomes interiorized and precious. I remember when I first visited such a hut in the Pentland hills near Edinburgh some fifteen years ago. The brother who took me there opened up the hut which was dedicated to St Seraphim, the 19th century Russian hermit. I noticed the small icon of Seraphim inside the door and asked why it was not outside. I recall his answer and searching look as he said. 'The King's daughter is all-glorious *within*!'[9] I got the message!

The group will feel a common, mutual and pastoral

responsibility for the hut and for the group members. This will mean that the families with children will have baby-sitters to enable them to make their monthly retreat, and that other kinds of sharing will take place in the *koinonia* (fellowship-sharing) of the Body of Christ. There will be a mutuality of joys and difficulties, and the learning process will be both personal and corporate.

It will be clear from the onset that some will want to share what has been happening to them in the light of this hut-spirituality. I cannot but be enthusiastic about it all, for even as I wrote the above paragraph about the Pentland hills hut, the longing for the hut in the wilderness sweeps over me again. Perhaps it is because my own Celtic roots find their nourishment in such a hut in the mystery of God's love that I feel such a response. Another thing that the brother said to me when I entered the hut where I lived for an academic year as I commented on its smallness (6' × 4'!), was: 'The next smallest thing you'll get to this is your coffin!' The brother himself is something of a desert father, and certainly his words, even of rebuke, were *verba salus*, words of salvation.

Thus it may feel right to keep a common journal and to meet perhaps monthly as a group so that there may be voluntary sharing of the hut experiences. Do not build expectations in this respect, for boredom and tedium may be the most important matters to be lived through and faced. There may be periods of what the Orthodox would call *enstasis* and *ekstasis*. *Enstasis* is a standing inside of oneself, finding the root, the centre, the deepest reality of one's being in God. *Ekstasis* is the experience of being taken out of oneself, being beside oneself in inebriation and joy.

There will also occur periods of desolation. When one is exposed to God in solitude, and seeks to descend into one's own depths, there is sometimes an upsurge of terror from the unconscious which spills over into the conscious. It may be a greater sense of one's finitude and mortality than ever experienced previously, or a realization of all the potential and actual darkness within, which has never truly been confronted before. We shall say a little of this later in speaking of mystical prayer, but it becomes necessary to have a supporting group, a spiritual father or mother, or a soul-friend to whom one can relate in joy or terror. 'It is a fearful thing to fall into the hands of the living God,' says the writer to the Hebrews. The fire of God is a flame which burns and scorches in purgation, like a crucible of gold being purified and refined of dross,[10] as well as being a fire which warms, enthuses and radiates the divine love and glory.

If you think the erection of such a hut in surroundings of beauty and solitude, with its place of quiet, study and prayer is a haven of delight, then practice will correct your thinking. It may indeed become an antechamber of heaven, but it will also become the furnace in which Shadrach, Meshach and Abednego were cast. But this furnace is fiery with the burning judgment of God, the purging fire of the divine Love, which consumes dross and refines gold to reflect His image and glory.

Hut spirituality is no novel idea. When I was first introduced into the actual practice and living of such a life, it was very hard, and yet I felt that my roots were in such soil, and that there was a rightness about it. We have such a hut in the monastery in which I now live, and whenever I go down to it, for a brief visit or a few nights, I feel again the quickening of my heartbeat, and my longing drawn out toward God, and a sighing and yearning in my heart for the Beloved in solitude. It is true that one carries the indwelling Christ within, wherever one is geographically. Yet there are holy places, made sacred by prayer and dedication, and there the Lord elects to manifest His Universal presence in a particular way. It is not just a communication of ideas, of theological know-how, but a revelation of the living God, an unveiling of His glory, so that one is struck by His beauty, his wonder, his splendour, and filled with holy fear by the radiance of his outshining.[11]

Poustinia: A Hut in the Desert

We have noted that hut spirituality has Christian and pre-Christian roots. In the Elijah and Elisha cycle of stories the 'sons of the prophets' were a kind of monastic and charismatic element in the life of ancient Israel who lived in wooden dwellings. Hut spirituality calls to mind the nomadic aspect of the pilgrim people of God dwelling in tents and having no permanent abiding place on earth because their citizenship was in heaven.[12]

The desert fathers of Palestine, Syria and Egypt lived in caves, wattle huts or stone and wooden dwellings, and so did the Celtic monks and hermits of our own islands from the 4th century or earlier. The Orthodox tradition has retained the hermit life in its fullness without any break, and it is significant that a popular paperback published a few years back about this hut spirituality of the *poustinia* (Russian for 'desert'), and the *poustinik* (person dwelling in a *poustinia*), comes from the pen of a Russian woman with an Orthodox and Catholic background.[13]

Catherine Kolyschkine was born into the spirituality of the Russian tradition in 1900, and escaped to the west in 1920 penniless, with her husband and baby son. Her gifts and lecturing soon made her wealthy, but in the midst of her new affluence she heard the words of Jesus: 'Sell all you possess, and give it to the poor, and come, follow me.' So now a widow, she provided for her son's education, sold up the rest, and went to live and work in the slums of Toronto. The story is exciting, full of anguish, waiting and obedience. But basically it is the story of silence of the desert and of prayer. And the centre of it is the development of the *poustinia*, a hut spirituality, and the establishment in the West of the vocation of the *poustinik*. Catherine feels it to have been newly rooted in the United States and Canada from Orthodox Russia, but I recognize in her descriptions of the place and the person, a continuity of the Celtic spirituality of the simple and austere gospel life of the monks and hermits of our own islands.

But be that as it may, if you have already found this

chapter applicable to your needs, providing a place and a time for meditative and contemplative prayer, then you should read this book, *Poustinia*. I shall develop in the remaining paragraphs, the idea of a *poustinik* as described by Catherine which will indicate the possibilities of a viable spirituality for the reader.

A *poustinik* could be fully a hermit, but with a door open to those who come in need, or one who spends periods of time in the *poustinia*. It could be a man or a woman, peasant or duke, learned or unlearned. It was considered a definite vocation, and often had a ministry of discernment or spiritual counsel within the vocation. She makes the point that the *poustinik* seemed to be more available than our idea of a hermit. There was a kind of gracious hospitality which was always open, and he had a 'welcome' face. He was a person of few words, but with great listening ability, and a deep understanding that loved without demanding anything for himself.

It is psychologically interesting that though they were called elder or wise one (staretz/staritaz), they often went into the *poustinia* around the age of thirty to thirty-five. But there were also some who had been married, reared their children, and then felt the pull of the desert.

Catherine makes the point that it was God who raised up such people. As the Russians said, he or she would arise and go into the place 'where heaven meets earth', leaving without any worldly goods, in the simple pilgrim's garment of a handwoven shift of linen down to the ankles, tied with a cord. Some would take leave of everyone in the village, but others would steal off in the night or at dawn, to pray for their sins and the sins of the world, to fast, live in poverty and enter the deep silence of God. She tells a beautiful and rather romantic, though austere, true story of a rich and noble man, Peter, a friend of her father's who had such a vocation. But I shall leave you to find and read the story for yourself in the chapter entitled 'Poustinia and Poustinik'.

The one further point I would like to pick up from Catherine and apply to the hut spirituality which I have outlined briefly, is that no one would dream of going off on his own, without the blessing and approval of the Church. This was not a sect mentality, a private revelation, an individualistic ego trip. Anyone who goes off into the desert on a whim of his own, whether on account of twisted narcissism, hatred or disappointment with the world, or as a reaction against a rejection in a relationship, is in for a terrible shock, or even an anguish that will lead to madness. In my scrapbook I have a quotation headed 'On the Sahara' written by someone who evidently knew what he was talking about. It runs:

> A sick heart finds no more effective cure in the desert than anywhere else; rather less, probably. The image of the man who is made a 'Saharan' by duty, by resentment, or by despair is entirely false. To picture the desert as a convalescent home or a place to retire to – what a misconception that is! The desert enriches only those who are already rich. It strengthens only the strong. One must entrust to it the heart's abundance and the mind's vitality; for these it brings to fruition.

It is certain that unless a pianist gives time and space to practice he will not truly play; unless a writer saturates himself with literature, he will not truly write; unless a potter gives hand and heart to his clay, he will not truly centre; unless a lover gives himself body and soul to his beloved, he will not truly love. So what does this say about prayer and God?

References

1 Jeremiah 18:1–6
2 *The Principles of the First Order of the Society of Saint Francis*, Day 16
3 1 Cor. 12 *passim*; Ephes. 4:1–14
4 James 5:14–16

5 Paul Tillich, *A History of Christian Thought*, pp. 1 f.
London: (SCM, 1968).
6 Mark 1:5; Matt. 26:18
7 Isa. 40:31; 2 Tim. 4:6
8 2 Kings 6:1,2
9 Ps. 45:13
10 Heb. 10:31
11 Exod. 33:17–23
12 Heb. 11:13–16; Phil. 3:20
13 Catherine de Hueck Doherty, *Poustinia*, Glasgow:
(Collins, 1977).

Part III: Exposure

9: Cosmic Prayer

The Deeper Reaches of Prayer

This chapter begins the section in which prayer is thought of as exposure to the holiness and love of God, leading to ever deepening union with him. Such a path is open to every Christian, but there are comparatively few who take it. It is a more concentrated awareness of the experience of God in creation and redemption and cannot operate within a dualism which separates the two. The major theme of the Gospel is reconciliation, and there must be such a reconciliation between man and God in conversion, but also between nature and grace in the life of prayer.

Exposure to the mystery of God in prayer opens up the depths of man's spirit to the Spirit of God. Such divine movement within the human person is both searing and inebriating, and the story of such exposure is indicated in these last chapters. It is God's will that the whole created order be reconciled to him in the union of love, so that God may be all in all.[1] The beginnings of such union are found on the path of cosmic and mystical prayer, and may be thought of as the deeper reaches of prayer.

The opening chapter of this book began with my childhood experience of the intuitive awareness of some kind of unitive mystery. As a child I felt this mystery above and beyond me, but also within me. I have since learned to use words like *transcendent* and *immanent* to describe such experience, but the using of philosophical words does not necessarily communicate the experience!

The fact is that to describe such experience of God is rather like describing the glory of a sunset or a symphony. If the hearers are colour-blind or tone-deaf the description may be eloquent, but the matter is not communicated. The assumption of this book is that there is an awareness of spiritual colour and tone, and that the basic stuff of spirituality, of God-awareness, is already inherent within the reader.

Cosmic prayer indicates that the created order is alive with the dynamic presence of God, with the invitation to deepen personal awareness of this presence. It leads to what I term *unitive experience* – which means that wherever I begin in the world of nature and humanity is the end of a golden string which leads me deeper into myself and into the mystery of God.

We are too familiar with the word *God* and yet unfamiliar with God-awareness, and the mystery of the divine depth. We do not necessarily come to know God by learning things *about* him – indeed scholastic, head-knowledge is counter-productive. It is by the experience of prayer and meditation that we come to *know* Him. He draws us deeper into prayer if we are open and passive in his hands, and the deeper we are drawn, the more dazzling is the radiance of His mystery.

Depth and Mystery

Today I went for a swim in the lake a few fields away from the monastery. There is an abundance of reeds all around the lake, and a lot of growth over the surface and into the depths. I have never touched the bottom so I don't know how deep it is. I dived into the beautiful coolness of the water on this hot summer day, and emerging from the depths felt the superficial warmth of the lake surface. The deeper it goes the colder it is, and the more mysterious. I love swimming in the lake, but if the truth be known, I am also scared of it. It is broad and wide and very deep. Because I don't *know* the depth, the mystery is unplumbable, and the growth which emerges from the depths and coils its tentacles around arms, legs and trunk makes me push it away to clear a wide area in which to float and swim.

I float on my back and look at the sky; I feel the warmth

and welcome of its embrace; I immerse myself and surrender to its mystery. I feel a little scared because I am alone, and I reflect on the mystery which I have been describing above. There is no need for me to press the application of the lake analogy, is there? There is something profound and beyond and within, something within myself which corresponds to the superficial light and warmth and to the scary, mysterious depths. I love the lake both for its refreshing coolness and for its deep, dark mystery. It is threatening because I could drown in it. I am enough at home in the watery element to float and swim and thrash about with joy. But the element is threatening enough to submerge me in fear and terror, and drag me into its watery depths.

I know a little about water, but the more I learn about it in chemical or biological terms and the more I experience it by being immersed in it, as in the experience of lake or sea, so the more it awes, intrigues and terrifies me. There are swimmers, better than I, whose 'fear-threshold' is higher than mine. But I know that if they were suddenly caught by cramp, cardiac fibrillation, or touched by a creature from the depths, they too would experience a terror akin to mine. Such is the mystery of God.

That lake experience is an illustration of cosmic prayer – learning by experience something of the mystery of God by an immersion in the creative process. I find myself more and more returning to childhood and nature in my experience of prayer, recovering a childhood cosmic vision which had grown dim. In the rest of this chapter I want to develop the cosmic prayer theme which operates from a wider perspective and a more profound understanding of nature and grace than is often found in the Western Church with its fear of nature and its domesticated Jesus.

Spending twelve months in solitude, in the summer beauty of Dorset and in the bleak wildness of a winter on the tip of the Lleyn Peninsula, sharpened my awareness of the cosmic dimensions of prayer. As well as my *Reflections on Solitude* which was a kind of *apologia* for solitary prayer, I also wrote an extended poem called *Cosmic Prayer*. It is in four sections and is included in the appendix so that it can be referred to as I now deal with the sections in turn.

Unity and Harmony

First of all there is the affirmation that the created order is a manifestation of the divine life. This is based on human experience and the revelation of the Gospel. Both nature and man are caught up in the cosmic catastrophe which theologians call The Fall. It is an existential fact that man and nature are in a state of disintegration and disharmony, but there is something which, even in the Eden story, antedates the fallenness of man and creation – and that is the primal state of innocence. Original innocence is the basic Christian doctrine, not original sin! Nevertheless, every man is Adam and every woman Eve. There is a personal awareness of a corporate disease, but we only know this because of our deeper awareness of an original innocence, harmony and union with the vital source of all things.

In cosmic prayer, those primal glimpses, those immortal longings, that divine restlessness, are touched by the universal love. And when such divine touches take place, when the prayer of the heart is the trysting place of meeting with God, we find our true selves in him, and begin to relate to the cosmos in a way that is reminiscent of *Paradise Regained* – the state of innocence in Eden.

It is quite easy to see why such an innocent and paradisical state is better glimpsed in childhood. The sad thing is that so many people grow away from their early intuitive knowledge. Henry Vaughan laments his fall from such childhood innocence when he glimpsed the face of God, and in his poem *The Retreat*, longs to return again:

> And looking back – at that short space –
> Could see a glimpse of His Bright face:
> When on some gilded cloud, or flow'r,

My gazing soul would dwell an hour,
And in those weaker glories spy
Some shadows of eternity:
Before I taught my tongue to wound
My Conscience with a sinful sound,
Or had the black art to dispense
A several sin to ev'ry sense,
But felt through all this fleshly dress
Bright shoots of everlastingness.

The very title of Wordsworth's poem on the theme expresses just what we are saying: *Intimations of Immortality from Recollections of Early Childhood*. A few lines express it:

. . . Heaven lies about us in our infancy!
Shades of the prison-house begin to close
Upon the growing boy,
But he beholds the light, and whence it flows,
He sees it in his joy . . .

. . . At length the man perceives it die away,
And fade into the light of common day.

Memories and recollections of such mystical vision have stayed with me. There has never been a time when the divine mystery has not communicated itself in the world of nature. Sometimes in heaviness and lonely yearning have I felt it, sometimes in Vaughan's 'bright shoots of everlastingness'. The creative Spirit has always communicated His presence.

So it is that the first thing that I was aware of as a child, and the primary recollection of cosmic prayer is the universal integration, pattern, regularity and harmonious movement of the natural world, which was, and is, reflected and re-echoed in the cave of my interior mystical life. It is something which embraces the whole of my being, body, soul and spirit, so that the prayer of St Paul is fulfilled in *soma*, *psyche* and *pneuma*.[2]

The Bondage of Creation

The second section of the poem speaks of creation's bondage, and indicates the reverberating echoes of the alienation of the human heart in the groaning travail of a created order that is frustrated within itself. There are constant echoes not only of the Eden story of innocence and fall, but also of the bondage and travail of creation in the Pauline theology of cosmic fall and redemption.[3]

Edenic Paradise and the state of innocence may have been the primordial fact, but the Genesis story depicts the break-up of the pattern in which there is a progressive alienating process. Adam feels the shadow in his own heart, followed by a breakdown of communication between himself and Eve with mutual blame, distrust and shame, and then the consequential alienation between man and God and the expulsion from Eden. This is no mere individual or domestic matter. Its reverberations are felt throughout the cosmic order, so that the whole creation groans in the travail of bondage and frustration.

The primary awareness in cosmic prayer is the divine harmony and unity, but the next moment one is plunged into the depths of darkness in which the shadows of alienation, disobedience, pride and the cosmic pain are manifest.

Cosmic finitude, transitoriness and mortality are not the only signs of restlessness in creation. It is more serious than that. It is a matter also of sinfulness, of alienation, and of the rational and logical destructive powers which have been unleashed upon the world, and but for the mercy of God, may catapult us into nuclear, apocalyptic catastrophe and the wholesale destruction of the human species.

Men and women of prayer are called to identify themselves with the dying Christ in His passion and with the risen Christ in His glory. He has accomplished in His cross and passion an objective work of atonement, and by His resurrection has unleashed the stronger, deeper powers of immortality and life.

Healing Through Suffering

The third section of the poem portrays Christ as the cosmic Lord who both suffers in his world and infuses life, light and love throughout the created order. Cosmic prayer is, therefore, an identification with Christ in his suffering, glory, and cosmic lordship. The Pauline metaphor of being 'in Christ' is an identification with him as the Second Adam who descends into the suffering and death of Gethsemane and Calvary to redeem and restore the lost paradise. It is the realization in experience that Christ restores in the man or woman of prayer a pristine innocence, that regeneration of the broken image, that restoration of the lost likeness which once reflected the glory of the creator. It is a path of prayer which cannot be entered into lightly, but only after much reflection and inward compulsion. It means such identification with the suffering servant of prophecy and ancient yearning[4] that the very being of the believer seems threatened. Identification in mystical union with Christ for the believer and for the Church is to enter into joy and glory, but it leads through the path of vicarious suffering for others, weeping and sweating in Gethsemane, and experiencing the desolation of the cry from the cross: 'My God, my God, why have you forsaken me?'[5]

When St Francis drew near to Mount Alverna towards the end of his life he knew what lay before him, and desired only one thing – that he might enter more deeply into the pain and love of Calvary. He longed to be completely identified with Christ in his dark and glorious passion – to feel His pain, to enter His darkness and to rise into His glory. Those days were the darkest of his life and that pain was the supreme moment of his existence. The excruciating terror and piercing of his body in the stigmata was also the complete identification in Jesus' death and resurrection.

This path to glory leads necessarily through the cross – there is no other way. But once that is understood and undertaken in utmost dedication, from that same cross shines a radiance, a healing light, a soothing balm which transfigures not only the body of Jesus, but the life of the believer and the whole cosmos with the promise of full redemption.

The way of Jesus always leads to the Father, and the path of Jesus' humanity always leads to the divine mystery which is at the heart of all things. The Father loves the Son and gives all things into his hands, pouring upon him, without measure, the gift of the Holy Spirit.[6] The Holy Spirit is the bond of union between the Father and the Son, and it is the glory of the Son to redeem the whole cosmic brokenness, to tread under foot the last enemy which is death, and to present to the Father the kingdom of love, so that God may be all in all.[7]

The Body of Christ

The Christ who is our Saviour, Redeemer and Brother is no domesticated, gentle Jesus. He is the Representative of the whole human race as true man, and also cosmic Lord, the Pantokrator, the mighty God. In the last section of the poem the Body of Christ is understood in three ways. It is first of all the human body in which the eternal Word became incarnate, the body prepared by the Father at the Incarnation.[8] In this body Jesus, the Christ, lived a radiant life of healing and compassion. In this body He suffered and died for the world's redemption. And in this body He was transfigured, raised and glorified, as the true pattern of our humanity.

Secondly the Body of Christ is the eucharist. His believing people are sustained by His body and blood, and they become members of his Body on earth by the power of the indwelling Spirit. Christ is the Head of that body – moving, actuating and guiding.[9] This is the third meaning of the term, and includes the whole company of the redeemed in earth and heaven.

This means that in that divine communication and communion between Christ and his Church, there is a mystical union of being, a participation in the divine life.[10] All the love, compassion, healing and reconciling power of the risen Christ is communicated to his believing Church corporately, and to its members individually. All those, therefore, who enter into the deeper reaches of prayer, meditating upon his person within the contemplative depths of shared being, actually become channels of the divine love to the world.

The risen and glorified Christ ascended to where He was before, in full communion and being with the Father and the Spirit, within the interpenetration of the divine life.[11] We, as individual believers and members of the Body of Christ, are drawn into actual participation in the life of the Holy Trinity. The Greek Fathers, following the mystical teaching of the New Testament, use the term *theosis* (divinisation) for such mystical sharing.[12] They mean, by this, not an impersonal pantheism, but a true sharing of the divine life, in which our isolation and individualism is overcome and caught up into the fullness and fountainhead of the Personal, finding our true identity in God, Father, Son and Holy Spirit.

This is the biblical and personal experience that is expressed in the four sections of the poem. It is not enough to read and assent to the theology, nor is it enough to glimpse and imagine the experience. There must be an actual participation which marries biblical theology to genuine experience of God, resulting in what we have called cosmic prayer.

Cosmic Prayer and Scripture

Cosmic prayer is grounded in a theology of creation and redemption and rooted in the created order and in the Scriptures of the Old and New Testaments. We shall round off this chapter by an illustration of the theme from one of the most powerful and significant chapters of the New Testament – the eighth chapter of Paul's letter to the Romans. So rich is the text that almost every translation has a further light to offer, but we shall be concerned especially with the verb and noun forms of the Greek word *stenazo* which bears the meaning, to sigh, to groan, to give vent to deep feelings of yearning, aspiration or anxiety.[13]

The word occurs three times in the chapter, in verses 22, 23 and 26, and is associated here and in other places with the travail of labour in childbirth,[14] used as an analogy of yearning prayer. The threefold repetition of the word with its maternal overtones is intimately connected with the feminine *ruach* or *Spirit* of God moving and breathing over the confusion of the primeval chaos, begetting form and life.[15] We shall examine the three verses separately, noting their contribution to the theme of cosmic prayer. Within the context of the letter to the Romans, they portray aspects of prayer which are rooted theologically and experientially in creation and redemption.

The Groaning of Creation

Verse 22 reads: 'We know that the whole creation has been *groaning* in travail together until now . . .' The groaning and travailing in this verse bear the prefix *sun-* before the verbs, indicating not only that there is such groaning and travailing, but that such a process occurs in all parts and elements of the created order, as the sound in the word '*sym-phony*'. Paul speaks of the man of prayer when he says: '*We* know . . .' for the man who has become aware, possessing the gift of discernment, can know and feel in mind and heart the sadness and yearning of the created order. This is what is meant by a *sym*pathetic and *com*passionate intuitive awareness of the sadness of our fallen world. It is not just an aesthetic gathering of all the poetry, music, art and literature which depicts the sadness of autumn dying and cosmic finitude, but it is also the sense of alienation which enters and mingles with the sad beauty.

There is a wistful and beautiful sadness about the rising and setting of the sun, the waxing and waning of the moon, the ebb and flow of the tides, the changing of the seasons. But to see the stone statue of Cain in the tropical greenhouse at Glasgow's Botanical Gardens, with the mark of alienation upon him is a deeper sadness. Lord Byron, in his thirty-third year used the language of nature-finitude to describe his moral condition:

> My days are in the yellow leaf,
> The flowers and fruits of love are gone;

The worm, the canker and the grief
Are mine alone.

Thus nature in all its parts groans and travails, and the impetus towards this fulfilment-yearning is the presence of the Holy Spirit at the heart of the created order. The man of prayer feels the reverberations of this within his own hidden depths.

We Ourselves Groan Inwardly
Verse 23 continues: '. . . and not only the creation, but we ourselves, who have the firstfruits of the Spirit, groan inwardly as we wait for . . . the redemption of our bodies.' The redemption that is in view here is bodily as well as spiritual. Paul uses not the *sarx* word for flesh in its alienated, fallen state, but the *soma* word for body in view of full redemption. The groaning of creation is not a rational concept but a body-mind participation. We ourselves, groaning in our inmost being, share the groaning and crying for redemption, completion, fulfilment. Paul has affirmed that this is a universal and cosmic groaning, for the whole universe is the object of God's creative love. But here he particularises and speaks of the Body of Christ: those who have received the Holy Spirit and yet are not fully redeemed. They are children of the firstfruits, yearning for the full harvest, groaning for the fullness of God in such union with the divine Love that God may be all in all.[16]

The Spirit Intercedes with Groanings
And so we come to the heart of the matter. The whole creation groans in all its parts, manifested in changing seasons, dying and rising, and yearning for fulfilment. We ourselves are an integral part of the created order and feel within ourselves the reverberation of creation's frustration, its finitude, transitoriness and mortality. All this, according to Paul, is grounded in the immanent and transcendent Spirit of God, and then, using the word for the third time in this passage he uncovers the root and

ground of all mystical prayer, in verses 26 and 27:

> Likewise the Spirit helps us in our weakness; for we do
> not know how to pray as we ought, but the Spirit
> himself intercedes for us with *sighs too deep for words*.
> And he who searches the hearts of men knows what
> is the mind of the Spirit, because the Spirit intercedes
> for the saints according to the will of God.

As Mother Julian says, 'God is the ground of our
beseeching.' In our inherent weakness we know neither
the matter or method of prayer, but can only groan and
sigh with creation. But the Holy Spirit who dwells in the
deepest cave of our heart, the temple of God, is also the
Spirit who searches the deep things of God.[17] The Spirit
within cries to the Spirit above. This is not liturgical
prayer, nor charismatic prayer, nor the gift of glossolalia
or the tongues of angels, but what the Authorized
Version, following closely the language of Paul, renders
'groanings which cannot be uttered'.

This is the kind of cosmic prayer into which we are
drawn. It is the universal groaning that all people of
wisdom and intuition feel, whether or not they are
Christians. It is the groaning of the believer who has
tasted the redeeming love of Christ and groans in longing
for its fulfilment. But more than all, it is the profoundly
interior work of the Holy Spirit, crying, groaning, sighing
and yearning – beyond all description, beyond all
knowing, beyond all imagining, in unutterable groanings
which burden the believer with intense joy and strange,
deep sadness.

I said at the beginning of this chapter that I glimpsed
these things in childhood. I have done a kind of full circle
and have been brought round to them again. It is a
retracing of my pilgrimage at a higher level, or a deeper
depth – we soon find ourselves in the difficulties of spatial
and analogical language again. That is why the deep,
secret and most profound language of the Holy Spirit is of
unutterable groanings within the infinite silence of God.

References

1 1 Cor. 15:28
2 1 Thess. 5:23
3 Romans 8:18–23
4 Isaiah 52:13–53
5 Matt. 27:46
6 John 3:34, 35
7 1 Cor. 15:28
8 Heb. 2:14–18; 10:5
9 Matt. 26:26–29; John 6:52–56; 1 Cor. 11:23–30; 12:12–27
10 Gal. 2:20; 2 Pet. 1:4
11 John 6:62
12 John 17:20–26
13 Note the usage of the word in context in Mark 7.34; Acts 7:34; 2 Cor. 5:2,4; Rom. 8:22,23,26
14 Gal. 4:19
15 Gen. 1:1
16 Eph. 1:3–23; 1 Cor. 15:28
17 1 Cor. 2:10

10: Levels of Prayer

Degrees of Spirituality and Prayer

In reading the gospels and epistles of the New Testament one is aware of different states of degrees of spirituality. This is found not only among the different churches and groups (compare and contrast the Corinthian Galatian and Colossian churches, and the seven churches of the Apocalypse), but also among individuals. The division between what Paul calls the *sarkikoi* (fleshly or carnal Christians) and the *pneumatikoi* (spiritual Christians)[1] may not be a difference of kind, but is certainly one of degree. The foundation is always secure, for that is Christ, but the edifice or superstructure which is built upon it reflects the quality of a Christian's carnality or spirituality. The purging of fire of God's love and judgment will test this material when all is made manifest in the day of Christ. [2]

So it is in the life of prayer. There are those who are merely sensual, still infants in Christ and only able to receive milk, unweaned, immature, even stunted in growth and unable to sustain solid food. Some of us have not moved beyond the 'petitionary prayer' stage which we learned as children, and have strange and immature ideas about prayer, about changing God's mind, about presenting our own wills to God for his approval. And God will have none of it! The life of prayer is a gradual and increasing surrender of our carnality and pseudo-ego to the divine will. It is a deeper penetration into the being of God by the Holy Spirit until we are caught up completely into the divine glory.

We shall deal more with these aspects in the next chapter, but just now I want to present part of a longer meditation on the levels or degrees of prayer which came to me during and after an early morning walk on the Anelog mountain just after dawn one January morning. As soon as the darkness gave way to light I felt impelled to walk around the tip of the peninsula in order to allow the content of the meditation to flow gently into my consciousness. The previous day I had been quietly aware of the Lord communicating His love, and whenever that happens, I try to be open, available, and recollected within myself so that I do not set up obstacles to receptivity. It is a matter of realizing in experience that although the Holy Spirit is powerful as wind and fire, yet there is that graciousness and gentleness about Him which is easily quenched and grieved. Let me now take up the writing from that early morning, building upon the primary experience recorded in my journal.

I am aware of the various levels or modes of awareness of the Lord's presence that come to me at different times. Yesterday, for instance, I sat busily at the table preparing a piece of calligraphy when I was gently but firmly arrested by what I can only call a 'sense of presence'. I was called and held for some little time, then released, and in the simple awareness of such a loving visitation, went on with my work. Moments or periods like this come without particular invitation. They last a brief time or are occasionally prolonged, and then the ordinary flow continues, enabling me to get on with the work in hand. Such periods are of sheer grace, their giftlike quality cannot be summoned or demanded; the most one can do is to desire to be open, make oneself ready, for it is at the will of the Beloved that the lover is visited.

This morning, especially, I have been aware of the three distinctions I make in the appropriation of the Lord's presence and love which flow from a disciplined life of prayer. They are distinctions whose edges are blurred and which sometimes flow into one another. But they do serve to distinguish between particular states which occur in my experience. Simply, they may be described in terms of my relationship to God the Beloved, as:

1 Learning *about* Him	–	Edification
2 Gazing *upon* Him	–	Meditation
3 Dwelling *within* Him	–	Contemplation

These three distinctions are incorporated into a deepening experiential knowledge of God. The verb 'to know' in the Old Testament is used of profound, intimate awareness of, and communion with, another in personal relationship. It is used frequently of sexual intercourse.[3] When used of relationship with God, therefore, the analogy is transformed into a mystical knowing which is quite different from academic knowledge. It is in the sphere of wisdom rather than scholastic attainment. This knowing of God is intuitive and experiential, and is only brought about by the interior work of the Holy Spirit. Even the first of the above degrees has more to do with intuitive and affective knowledge than with intellectual, objective knowledge. Let me take them separately.

1 Learning *about* Him: Edification

Conversion to Christ may be of the nature of 'love at first sight', as it was on the Damascus Road when Saul of Tarsus was struck, maimed, and forever wounded by the divine Love. His first words were: 'Who are you, Lord?'[4] In any loving relationship the lover seeks to know more of the beloved. So whether the knowledge of the Lord is a sudden conversion or a gentle, continuing process,[5] it is an interior knowledge of the heart, and not a cerebral recognition of facts. The mind, of course, is involved, for the knowledge is of the whole person.

Learning *about* God we have marked as 'edification'. This is a New Testament word which has to do with building – the erection of an edifice. Our learning 'about' the Lord is a building up of an interior knowledge of His grace, His love, His providential care. It is an ever more intimate delving into that lore of spiritual knowledge which is found in Scripture, in the fellowship of the Church and in the world, which reflects the glories of the Beloved. The discipline of learning is involved, and the beautiful invitation which illustrates this is found in Matthew's Gospel: 'Come to me all who labour and are heavy laden, and I will give you rest. Take my yoke upon you and learn from me; for I am gentle and lowly in heart, and you will find rest for your souls. For my yoke is easy, and my burden is light.'[6]

The learning process may well include intellectual effort; it may demand hours of intense study, perhaps even a course in New Testament Greek! But it is the edifying learning about God which builds up the believer in the knowledge and love of God. No disciplined and intellectual study is to be despised in this respect, as long as it is in the spirit of humble dedication. To illustrate the blurred edge where learning *about* our Lord runs over into meditation, gazing *upon* Him, it may be a profitable exercise to do a simple act of serious Bible-study which spontaneously develops into prayer.

Look, for instance, at William Barclay's treatment of a simple Greek word in his commentary on 2 Timothy 4:6:

I am already on the point of being sacrificed; the time of my departure (*analusis*) has come. I have fought the good fight, I have finished the race, I have kept the faith . . .

Barclay makes the point that the Greek word Paul chooses for 'departure' *analusis*, is a word which in common usage depicted:

1 the unyoking (*analusis*) of an animal from the shafts of its plough or cart when the labour of the day is done;
2 the loosening (*analusis*) of bonds or fetters when a prisoner gains his longed-for liberty;
3 the pulling up (*analusis*) of tent ropes and pegs when the pilgrimage moves on;
4 the letting go (*analusis*) of the mooring ropes of the ship when it is ready to sail out of the harbour and into the open sea.

Paul is speaking of the setting free (*analusis*) of the soul from the body and the anticipation of meeting his Lord. It is clear how mind and heart combine in such a study of the text, bringing the believer into such loving communion with the Lord of Scripture that edification moves easily into meditation.

2 Gazing *upon* Him: Meditation

We move now from the study to the prayer-cell, or to that place of prayer in solitude which is bounded by earth, sea and sky. This does not mean, of course, that moments of adoration may not break in upon the enlightened student. It is possible to bury oneself in a lexicon and to arise in the presence of God. Nevertheless, meditation is more appropriate in a posture of prayer than surrounded by the appendages of intellectual study. There is a way of reflective reading which is conducive to a state of absorbed meditation upon God. I am not thinking now of the prophetic word which pierces to the heart and produces conviction and repentance. That certainly is basic to the believer and of primary significance. But I am thinking of the desire of the converted believer, the lover of God, to draw near in devotional and reflective meditation – gazing upon the Beloved.

When the lover receives a letter from his beloved, or looks upon her photographs or a gift she has given him, he will meditate upon her loveliness. He will not only recall the qualities which reflect the beauty of her mind and body, but upon the very nature of her being, that mingling of their lives in which the well-spring of love bubbles up to the mutual delight of one another.

To meditate upon the qualities of the beloved brings one to the borderland of mystical prayer where Scripture, mystical theology, devotional classics, hymnology, poetry, the beauty of the created order and the whole gamut of positive human relations remind one of the Beloved. Ramon Lull, the thirteenth century Franciscan, in his *Book of the Lover and the Beloved*, is carried away by such an analogy:

The Lover went in desire of his Beloved, and he met two friends who greeted and embraced and kissed each other with love and tears. And the Lover swooned, so strongly did these two lovers call his Beloved to mind.[7]

The devotional classics of both the catholic and evangelical traditions are full of the mutual love which indwells the believer and his Lord, drawing deeply on the analogy of human love. St Bernard's sermons on the Song of Songs are an extended meditation on the loveliness of God in Christ, and the poetry of St John of the Cross catches the experiential wonder of the soul caught up in meditative adoration of the Beloved. Meditation in the light of the Holy Spirit stimulates yearning in the heart of the believer. On the pattern and analogy of human love, meditative prayer in love leads to yearning for union with the beloved. Take this secular love poem:

> When I take fire from you
> All my limbs tremble;
> Head, heart and hand catch flame
> None can dissemble;
> For that pure tongue of fire
> Darkness dispelling
> Pierces my blackest night
> Radiance indwelling.
>
> When you take fire from me
> Strange beauty clothes you;
> Head, heart and hand are touched,
> And wisdom moves you;
> Reciprocated love
> Measure for measure
> Gives, takes accordingly
> Sharing its treasure.
>
> When mutual fire ignites
> In one flame burning,
> The fiery source is touched
> In utter yearning;

Then the co-mingled flame
Leaping still higher
Transforms our earthly heat
To heavenly fire.

When flame burns within flame
Of earth and heaven,
And two hearts burn as one
Unto love given,
Then fire will burn and glow
Darkness illuming,
In its pure, utmost heat
All else consuming.

The human analogy of love is rich in symbolic correlation with the love of God. Indeed the divine Love is love at its source, and the true mystic will bear witness that human love, which fulfils the depth of human yearning, still pales before the unutterable, ineffable glory and flame of the divine Love.

Following the human analogy, it is the experience of the believer that love inevitably follows the path of suffering for the Beloved. There is a darkness and an aridity that invades the yearning soul in searching for the Beloved, having glimpsed His glory; but that is forgotten in the ecstasy of the union of love when God touches and visits the soul. The suffering experienced by the soul is a participation in the love of Christ who suffered for his bride, the Church. In one of his contemplative poems St John of the Cross captures both the beauty and the pain of Christ's suffering love as a pattern of contemplative meditation:

A shepherd lad was mourning his distress,
Far from all comfort, friendless and forlorn.
He fixed his thought upon his shepherdess
Because his breast by love was sorely torn.

He did not weep that love had pierced him so,
Nor with self-pity that the shaft was shot
Though deep into his heart had sunk the blow,
It grieved him more that he had been forgot.

Only to think that he had been forgotten
By his sweet shepherdess with travail sore
He let his foes (in foreign lands begotten)
Gash the poor breast that love had gashed before.

'Alas, alas for him,' the shepherd cries,
'Who tries from me my dearest love to part
So that she does not gaze into my eyes
Or see that I am wounded to the heart.

Then after a long time a tree he scaled,
Opened his strong arms bravely wide apart,
And clung upon that tree till death prevailed
So sorely was he wounded in his heart.

The breast of Christ is pierced by love before it is pierced by his enemies, and the tenderness of his love unto death is communicated to his bride. Meditation on the glory and pain of the cross leads to the contemplative vision of union with God. Such a vision brought St Francis to the suffering of the stigmata in which he attained by grace to such union with Christ that the ecstasy of spiritual communion overflowed into his bodily members and he was marked with the wounds of the passion. So we are brought to the borderland of meditation and contemplation.

3 Dwelling *within* Him: Contemplation

The indwelling rest which is found in the Lord is a rest from the weight and burden of our sins, and a refuge in time of tribulation and persecution. But primarily and ultimately it is an interior resting in His love. It is the child resting on the breast of its mother,[8] the lover resting in the Beloved.[9] One of the stanzas of F. W. Faber's hymn on the majesty of God is criticized because misunderstood, but it carries this feeling of wonder and contemplative resting:

Father of Jesus, love's reward
What rapture will it be,
Prostrate before thy throne to lie
And gaze, and gaze on thee?

There are times when such an experience comes after long hours of waiting in darkness, yearning for a revelation of the tenderness of Christ. St John of the Cross portrays the soul as wounded by the love of Christ in conversion and the beginnings of contemplative prayer, and comments:

> The healing of the wounds of love comes only from him who inflicted the wounds. Hence the soul says that she went forth calling for him who dealt the wound, begging to be healed, crying out at the violence of the burning caused by the wound.[10]

This is the measure of prayer found in the contemplative way, where meditation is transformed into contemplative adoration and yearning, so that the believer thirsts ever more deeply for a more intimate union with God. It is a mutual yearning, initiated by the crucified Jesus when he cried out: 'I thirst.' The love of the bride and the bridegroom, and the yearning of one for the other are indicated again in St John of the Cross in the following paragraph from his commentary on the Spiritual Canticle:

> He who has fallen in love has been robbed or reft of his heart by the one whom he loves. For his heart strays far from him, set upon his beloved. And so he has no heart of his own, for it belongs to the one whom he loves. And so the soul can know whether or not it loves God; if it loves Him it will have no heart save for God only.[11]

And the mutuality of love's mingling between God and the soul is set forth beautifully when he says:

> The Bridegroom likens himself to a hart. Now the hart, as is well known, mounts to lofty places and when wounded seeks in all haste refreshment in cool waters. Moreover if it hears its mate complain and

sees she is wounded he immediately goes to her, caresses and fondles her. Even so the Bridegroom, seeing the bride wounded with love for him, comes when she sighs, wounded likewise with love for her; for when two love each other the wound of one is the wound of both.[12]

There are times, at this stage, when the love of God suddenly takes hold of the believer without any particular preparation on the believer's part. It is the surprise of the lover who suddenly approaches and catches away his beloved, and causes her to rest in him, so that they enjoy profound mutual indwelling.

Men and women who have related their experiences in the path of contemplative prayer indicate great variation in the divine initiative and human response. The contemplative way is a way of glory and of suffering. But always there is the profound interior resting within the love and mercy of God. Within this way there are many levels of the divine awareness and intimacy. The very word 'contemplation' is one which speaks of vision, of gazing upon the glory of God. This is what St John's words indicate: 'Beloved, we are God's children now; it does not yet appear what we shall be, but we know that when He appears we shall be like Him, for we shall see Him as He is.'[13] It is a transformation brought about by gazing upon the unutterable glory of God: 'And we all, with unveiled faces, beholding the glory of the Lord, are being changed into His likeness from one degree of glory to another; for this comes from the Lord, who is the Spirit.'[14]

The Three Levels

Learning *about* Him, gazing *upon* Him, dwelling *within* Him. These are the three levels, easy to remember, yet profound in their meaning and experience. The learning process of the heart is both spontaneous and disciplinated when the motivation is love. But such a process leads to a meditative attitude in which the whole of life is marked by a deeper awareness of the divine presence, and which opens up to the contemplative vision.

There is an inter-penetration of these modes or levels of learning, gazing and dwelling in the mutuality of prayer. Therefore no one ever arrives at the ultimate, but continually participates in the divine life, while the capacity for larger vision and union within the divine mystery of God reaches into infinity and eternity. 'Not that I have already obtained this or am already perfect; but I press on to make it my own, because Christ has made me his own.'[15]

References
1 1 Cor. 3:1–3
2 1 Cor. 3:1–17
3 Gen. 4:1,17; Matt. 1:25
4 Acts 9:5
5 2 Tim. 3:15
6 Matt. 11:28
7 Ramon Lull, *The Book of the Lover and the Beloved*, Meditation 59 (SPCK, 1978).
8 Psalm 131:2
9 Song of Songs 7:1–10
10 *Spiritual Canticle*, I, xi
11 *Ibid.*, IX, iv
12 *Ibid.*, XII, viii
13 1 John 3:2
14 2 Cor. 3:18
15 Phil. 3:12

11: Mystical Prayer

In this chapter I want to draw attention to three great interior movements in the life of prayer which have shaped the mystical tradition. They reflect the whole range of spirituality from the evangelical to the catholic traditions, and represent the heart of the Gospel in the life of prayer. These three movements are known as:

1 Purgation
2 Illumination
3 Union.

Mystical Prayer is the Gospel Within
By mystical prayer I mean that kind of communion with God, Father, Son and Holy Spirit in which the believer is drawn ever more deeply, from an elementary and basic affirmation of God, right through to the highest degree of glory possible on earth.

This means that mystical prayer is simply the Gospel applied to the inward life of the believer by the Holy Spirit, which overflows in an outward life of compassion and love. It means also that it is not the prerogative of a selected few, but is wide open to every Christian. The fact that few seem to respond at the level of God's will only indicates the narrowness of the way so that there are few who find it. 'Many are called but few are chosen'[1] certainly applies here, for the way is hard and the disciplines are inherent in the journey. This was quite clear in the early Church. To take up one's cross and follow Jesus was a costly thing. To cleave to the Gospel and throw in one's lot with the Church of the New Testament was risky and difficult and dangerous. The suffering we shall be talking about is mainly interior, psychological and spiritual, but in the early Church (and today in various parts of the world) to affirm the way of Jesus was politically and socially unacceptable, leading to persecution or martyrdom.

Mystical prayer will certainly lead us to a compassionate sharing in the sufferings of others both physical and spiritual, but we are primarily concerned with the interior sufferings on the path of prayer which are the consequence of our taking the faltering responsive steps on the way to a deeper life of prayer in God. Such suffering will arise both from our own complicated and fallen situation, and from the influence of dark, cosmic powers. There is no evasion of suffering for it is the way the Master went. It led through the blood and sweat of Gethsemane, through the agony and passion of Calvary; but it led to glory. We shall examine each of the stages of the mystical path in turn, but shall see that they are not simply successive, but often concurrent. We shall also find that they are not simply repetitive, but recurring. By that I mean that they 'come around again' at a different level, rather like a spiral staircase which in retracing itself in a circular manner actually reaches ever higher levels. It is a pattern of purgation, illumination, union, which recurs, and continually breaks into new awarenesses of life, light and love.

Purgation

The mystical path begins with purgation, which in New Testament language is the penitence and repentance of the first movement towards God, the purifyng and purging from sin, and the progressive sanctification in which the believer is made over more and more from his old life, to the life of holiness and love.[2] The initial cleansing or purging from sin becomes a continual process on the way of sanctification, and the glory of the risen and ascended Christ is that the purging of sins was part of his objective work of atonement.[3] It is interesting that the Authorised Version translates the Greek word for the pruning-cleaning process in the analogy of the vine and the branches with the English verb 'to purge'.[4] This word *purgation* represents to us the activity of God the Holy Spirit in cleansing us from defilement and disease, burning out the dross, crucifying our lusts and evil desires and removing all the obstacles to growth in love and prayer. The way to God is simple, it is we who are complicated, and much of the purgation stage of prayer is dealing with the sophisticated and evasive complications which we set up, in order to cling to our sins, entanglements, carnal lusts and lesser loves. There is a searing pain involved in such a radical work, and most of us shrink from it at some point, and prefer to rest where we are, so that the next stage has to wait, either until some catastrophic illness, bereavement or circumstance throws us on to God in complete helplessness, or until after our death, when the journey continues into the infinite loving mystery of the Godhead.

Purgation is inseparable from illumination and glimpses of union, but let's stay with purgation for a moment. There is a certain joy in repentance – the New Testament word is *metanoia* which means, literally, a turning around of the mind or heart. The imperative form does not mean 'do penance', but 'change your heart', and there is an acknowledgment that unless God does the turning, we shall not be turned. When the initial purging process is over, we may rejoice in the respite and in the light of illumination, but we soon realize that sanctification is a life-work, and like an onion, we have numerous protective coats which have to be peeled off.

Prayer is a continual and deepening surrender to God, and there are frightening aspects to such a surrender. The great mystery of God is far removed from the sentimental old man in the sky image which some of us have carried for years. But it is also far removed from the despotic tyrant who searches you out to damn your soul which some theologies espouse. Thomas Merton's book, *Contemplative Prayer*, deals with the perpetual surrender and the psychological and spiritual evasions which we practice to keep God at bay, for we know the reality of God to be dangerous! He shows us that if we are seriously engaged on this pilgrimage of prayer, then we shall realize that we must be exposed to the true God who burns in inebriating love and in conflagrating judgment by the very same burning.

This is certainly a very good antidote to the 'matey' God of some undisciplined charismatic groups, though the true charisms of the Holy Spirit lead to the profound mystery of which we are speaking. Reverence, awe, fear of God in the depths of the soul are experiences which take place during this process of purgation. When Isaiah the prophet was carried in vision into the court of heaven and beheld such wonders he cried out: 'Woe is me! For I am lost; for I am a man of unclean lips, and I dwell in the midst of a people of unclean lips; for my eyes have seen the King, the Lord of hosts.'[5] Then came the purging, as the flaming seraph took a burning coal with tongs from the heavenly altar, and purified and purged the uncleannes of heart and mouth by touching Isaiah's lips with it.

The reverential awe and terror of the Old Testament in the manifested presence of the Lord is something which is lost to many contemporary people and to much of the Church, perhaps because it has been associated with the kind of negative and destructive Calvinism and Catholicism which cast sinners into hell from the anger of a petulant and irate deity. But the more one reads the Scriptures of the Old and New Testaments, and the more one peruses and experiences the mystical path in the steps of the great traditions of prayer down the ages, the more one realizes in one's own experience the awe and godly fear of the transcendent.

My own time of solitude contained much of this element of purgation, and the second period was much more stringent than the first in the exposure to the purging fire of the Holy Spirit. Complicated evasions and sheer funk in the presence of God gave rise to much existential pain and fear. The geographical and spiritual solitude afforded no escape, there were no diversions, no one to run to, no entertainments or scintillating company or theological argumentation to take my attention away from myself in the presence of the living God. And when I surrendered to the way God lured me into the wilderness,[6], and actively responded to him in the sanctifying work of purging love, then I found I could lie on the ground in tears and love, crying:

> O, how I fear thee, living God
>   With deepest, tenderest fears,
> And worship thee with trembling hope,
>   And penitential tears.

Social and Political Implications

Of course, one does not have to go off into a physical desert to know this experience. But it is very difficult to escape the web of illusion that is spun around modern man by the falsity of the pseudo-world of advertising and western sophistication which envelops us all in ways we are hardly aware of. When we come up against people who have seemingly opted out of our society negatively, many of us feel tinges of envy, and their freedom often makes us angry because we think they are not facing up to the reality of the real and contemporary world. And all the time we are too carnal, too lazy, too comfortable, too downright sinful to look at ourselves and our society, to consider seriously the western rape of the greater part of our poor world. We are armed to the teeth with catastrophic nuclear weapons in which, if the truth be known, we really put our trust, prepared for governments to finance such horrific destruction with millions of pounds and ultimately millions upon millions of people, to save our own miserable skins. And this is only part of the picture!

It is a modern version of the situation in which the desert fathers lived, in which they fled from the approved establishment of the Christian Church with its alliance with the world-system. They fled into the desert and actually organized an alternative society. A reading of Thomas Merton's *Wisdom of the Desert* together with Morris West's novel, *The Clowns of God*, bring before us, seventeen centuries apart, the pressure towards an alternative way of living and loving and reconciling, though the path lies through loneliness, suffering and rebirth, for it is the way of the cross.

The whole movement of purgation in the life of prayer is social and corporate as well as individual and monastic. These cannot really be separated, for as I am aware of a deepening of a vocation to the way of solitude for myself, I am more aware of my roots in the world, the church and the monastic community to which I belong. Other brothers and sisters in this community, while I am obeying the call of the Spirit into deeper ways of solitude and contemplation, are living, writing, walking and protesting; they are thinking, working and organizing, to bring the simplicity and reconciliation of the Gospel into the marketplace, into the cities, into the technological world. I am but a member of the whole body, and there are tremendous political and social repercussions to the revolutionary gospel of love, reconciliation and solitude to which we bear witness.

The point I am making is that there is taking place in my own life, through my own particular circumstances, a process of purgation which I want to share, and to which I want to lead others, so that they, in their turn, will allow such a vocation to spill over into witness and loving revolutionary change in the world. If it seems negative at this point, it is only because we have not passed in our thinking from purgation to illumination and union. But first there are some more things to be said.

The object of purgation in the life of prayer is that it prepares the soul for illumination and union with the divine Love. In other words, it prepares man for union with God who is his home, the fountainhead of his life and from whom he is cut off in an alienated world and society. It is the work of salvation in its widest sense to restore man as an individual and as a species, to his inheritance, in which the world is charged with the glory and splendour of God as creator and redeemer. Here are the beginnings of an existential and political revolution which has its roots in the loving, redeeming God. The world, made over into the image and likeness of God, will glorify God in its creativity, renewal and forgiving love. We shall need to contemporarize the old prophecies, and the way will be difficult, impossible, for the carnal man, but we shall be among those who 'beat their swords into ploughshares, and their spears into pruninghooks; nation shall not lift up sword against nation, neither shall they learn war any more'.[7]

The Dark Night

Before we leave this stage of purgation we must refer to what is called, in the mystical tradition, 'the dark night of the soul'. It is possible to become complicated, introspective and medieval in a pejorative sense at this point. There is a strange affinity, in some neurotic people, with such concepts as 'the dark night' when, in fact, they are seeking either an excusing evasion to facing the reality of their own situation, or are off on yet another ego trip which will give them the sense of identity and fulfilment they have been unable to find in normal human relations. Even saying this much indicates the perilous ground which is beneath our feet.

In speaking of the dark night of the soul, we mean that when the soul is exposed to the divine Light which is God, certain things happen. 'God is light', says St John, 'and in Him is no darkness at all.' This is a bit paradoxical because there is more than one Greek word for darkness. The New Testament word *skotos* usually has negative connotations in its metaphorical sense, but the word *gnophos* is another word for darkness which does not carry those negative meanings. It is appropriate, in John's Gospel, for Nicodemus to come to Jesus to find salvation by night, but when John says that Judas went out into the night, he means that Judas entered into the darkness of betrayal and death.[8] It is only a seeming paradox that the

183

time of darkness and night is often the best time for contemplative prayer in God who is light and radiance and glory and splendour. But it becomes clearer when one realizes what is happening.

The Judeo-Christian tradition bears witness to the ascent to God on contemplation as an advance into darkness, and writers like Gregory of Nyssa speak of the ascent of Moses into the cloud and darkness of Mount Sinai[9] as an analogy of the contemplative way. Gregory also associates this Sinai darkness of contemplative awareness of the mystery of God with the darkness and night of the Song of Songs. The darkness is the night in which love between lover and beloved is consummated. This is taken up by the Western tradition in St Bernard, St John of the Cross, and eventually finds its way into both catholic and evangelical spirituality of later times. So if we bear in mind the *gnophos* darkness which is neutral and does not bear the negative and evil connotations we sometimes associate with *skotos* darkness, then it is clear that we are not ascribing to God any quality which compromises the glory and radiance of His infinite love. Indeed, we may then speak of His dazzling darkness, and of his sending out a ray of darkness in which the soul is struck with the glory of the incomprehensibility of God.

Dazzling Darkness and Purgation

What then is this darkness, and what 'certain things' happen to the soul exposed to the dazzling reality of God? St John of the Cross tells us that the dark night is an inflowing of God into the soul which purges it from ignorance and imperfections. God thus secretly instructs the soul in the perfection of love while it does nothing other than waiting lovingly upon God, listening and receiving His light without understanding intellectually the means of such infused contemplation. He goes on to say that the loving wisdom of God produces striking effects in the soul, 'for by *purging* and *illumining* it, he prepares it for the *union* of love with God.'[10]

184

In this statement are mentioned the three stages of purgation, illumination and union, and it brings us to the borderland between purgation and illumination. The question which arises at this point is why such a state on the mystical path of contemplative prayer is called the dark night. St John answers that there are two reasons. First, the Divine Wisdom is so impenetrable and incomprehensible to the feeble human mind that to attempt to encompass such incomprehensibility is night and darkness to the soul, because the finite cannot comprehend the infinite. Secondly, the Divine Wisdom is also the Divine Holiness and Love; the soul in comparison is vile and impure, and therefore the darkness of the soul is affliction and torment.[11]

Following our image of the love of God as the hidden fire, we may say that the fierce conflagration of God's fiery love is a loving holiness and a holy love. It purifies the believing soul in the crucible of love, but it consumes the unbelieving soul in its fierce heat of judgment. It is the same sun that melts the wax that hardens the clay!

St John of the Cross uses analogies at this point, saying that if diseased eyes look into the sun, one does not impute darkness to the sun, but to the eyes' disease. Again, he says that if the Creator is teaching the creature, be it ever so gently, the vastness of the mystery throws the poor creature into the maze of incomprehensibility, and it even feels abandoned and grieved in the process.

This speaks of the problem of people who have been visited by God on this path of prayer when they feel 'amazed', lost in wonder, and even quite scared, in holy fear of God, because of both the frightening chasm between Creator and creature, and the immanent nearness of God within the soul. The quality of numinous and prostrating awe that seized the patriachs and prophets, and that suddenly shone forth from Jesus becomes quite clear at this point.[12] These aspects of God's holiness and incomprehensibility are not only woven into the fabric of Scripture, but are reflected in the fathers of the Church and the mystical tradition of prayer. And at a lower but just as real level, they are re-echoed in our liturgies and hymnology:

Eternal Light! Eternal Light! How pure the soul must be
To stand within thy searching sight
And shrink not, but with calm delight
Can live, and look on thee.

As we move on to the stage of illumination, it is worth noting two more comments of St John of the Cross. He says that when the soul suffers the direct assault of the divine light, the pain resulting from its impurity is immense because it is God's will to purge and sanctify it. The soul thus feels bombarded with the divine light, and has become sensitive in its misery, with grief and pain because it feels that God may cast it away. He goes on to say that it is a great wonder and pity that this is so because God is really being gentle and his dealings with the soul are light and merciful. It is not even chastisement, but healing remedy.[13]

This is why St John of the Cross is so keen that the believer should stay close to Scripture and to a reliable spiritual guide who knows the way. In both the catholic and reformed traditions we find periods of time in which men like Augustine, Francis of Assisi, Martin Luther, John Wesley, John Bunyan, and in our own day Thomas Merton, have been weighed down with the burden of their unlikeness to God. It is a matter both of their comparative impurity and of the wonder of the incomprehensibility of God. The Book of Job is full of the perplexity of his own creatureliness and sinfulness; Joseph was perplexed though trusting, from the moment he was cast into the pit by his brothers to the time he was called into Pharaoh's presence years later; Jonah wondered what was happening in the belly of the sea monster; the psalmist is caught up in great bewilderment, complaint and near despair; Jeremiah had times of great darkness and lamentation. The way of purgation is a hard and difficult way, but it is only one of the three elements of the mystical life of prayer.

Illumination

The purgative way has been called the way of beginners; the illuminative way the way of the proficient, and the unitive way the way of the perfect. This is categorically too rigid. The three elements, namely, the deepening of repentance, the growth of faith and widening of vision, and experiential union with God, are all present in the simplest and most basic Christian experience. But as we have said, there is a recurring return to these experiences at higher levels, and an intermingling of the stages as the believer grows in grace and loving knowledge of God in Christ. As long as one remembers these things, the threefold division is useful, for there are beginner, intermediate and advanced souls!

One of the excellent analogies St John of the Cross uses at this point is that of a log of damp wood and the process of its being taken up into the warmth, light and heat of the fire. He says that the divine light which acts upon the soul in purging and preparing it for perfect union acts as fire upon a log of wood in order to transform it into itself. Firstly, the fire begins to dry it, driving out and expelling the moisture. This makes it black and unsightly, and as it dries gradually it gives out a bad smell. But the process drives out all the unsightly accidents which are contrary to the nature of fire. As the process continues, the purging gives way to kindling, to warmth and heat, and finally there is the transformation into the beauty and wonder of its own nature – the log becomes the fire and the fire burns.[14]

The analogy is self-explanatory. In the beginning the fire's energies are concentrated on the purgation element rather than producing heat. But with persistence and yielding on the part of the soul, the divine fire begins to kindle warmth and heat so that there is a sensible awareness of the presence and activity of the divine Love. John quotes Psalm 39:3: 'My heart became hot within me. As I mused, the fire burned.'

The stage of illumination answers to faith and vision. Its spectrum is wide, from the first stirrings of believing trust in the heart of the repentant sinner, right through to the meditative depths of sharing with Jesus in the Gospels and gazing upon his loveliness in the glory of the Father. Primary illumination is the looking to Jesus crucified and risen as Saviour and Lord. It is an entering by experience into the riches of Scripture and the fellowship of the Church with its teaching and sacraments, all of which are received with joy and understanding. It is dynamic and not static because there is no reception of a body of doctrine without its felt application of heart and mind. The believer *feels* and *knows* the truth, participates in the joys and sorrows of the way of Jesus, and allows Gospel light to saturate his life and overflow in loving relationships. This is the state in which most believing Christians live out their Christian profession. The spectrum is very wide, so that there is a great body of teaching, discipline, discipleship and concrete application of the Gospel to be experienced and lived out. Also the life of prayer moves within the framework of liturgical and church worship in ministry and eucharist, and includes all basic forms of prayer up to the beginnings of meditation. The Christian learns to experience the difference between petition, thanksgiving, intercession, praise and adoration, and grows within the context of Scripture and his own particular tradition.

At this stage of illumination, the disciplines of moderate ascetical practice are also part of his rule of life, and some involvement in social concern is a consequence of following Christ. Problems begin when the Christian who has known the discipline of purgation and ongoing faith, is integrated into the life of the Church, and occupied with Christian Aid, CAFOD, Tear Fund or Amnesty International, etc., becomes either too busy in active charitable preoccupations or neglects the means of grace and allows the vision to grow dim.

But we shall suppose that there is a constant feeding of the divine fire within, and a discovery of the deepening life of prayer by waiting upon God and reliance upon the Holy Spirit. If the believer develops the life of prayer and gives himself to God in some of the ways of prayer we have described, with close attention to Scripture, then joy will be renewed, the purgation-illumination process will continue, and the pilgrimage will become both more demanding and more fulfilling. At one and the same time prayer will be an adventure into the deeper knowledge of God and a quest into the meaning and identity of one's own life.

The Cross

In the Christian life the cross has always been central, both as the means of our redemption and as the symbol of our dying and rising again in close identification with Christ.[15] The analogy of the log burning in the fire brought before us the paradox contained in the purgation-illumination stages, and this is the very thing that the cross effects in our lives. In the first chapter I quoted the poem on the cross from the *Lauda* of the 13th century Franciscan friar, Jacapone da Todi. The whole poem is reproduced in the appendix and an examination of it at this point will make it quite clear the tremendous joy and pain engendered by the same cross in the interchange between Jacapone's two friars. These two friars represent the two halves of the Christian who is committed to the Christ of Calvary. The dual purgation-illumination experience in the poem indicates that while the interior work of purgation continues without abatement, yet the illumination experience of joy, peace, awakening, proclamation, forgiveness, reconciliation and new life cause the second friar to laugh, shout and sing. There is the indication of glimpses, and more than glimpses, of the unitive life throughout the poem, and in the life and work of Jacapone himself there is this continual paradoxical mixture.

The Franciscan tradition as a whole is full of the glory and pain of the cross. Francis Bernadone, as a young man, was kneeling one day in the tumbledown church of San Damiano below Assisi, before a large Byzantine type crucifix, and he felt and heard the Christ speak and call to him from the cross to a life of discipleship. This life was filled with intense joy and profound sorrow, and Francis has been thought of as the man who followed Jesus more closely than any other outside the New Testament.

Certainly the last two years of his life were marked by the powerful experience of the stigmata at La Verna; the followers of Jesus in the Franciscan tradition have always rejoiced and sorrowed in the cross of Jesus, and still see it as St Paul saw it: 'The word of the cross is foolishness to those who are perishing, but to us who are being saved it is the power of God. . . . When I came to you brethren, I did not come proclaiming to you the testimony of God in lofty words or wisdom. For I decided to know nothing among you except Jesus Christ and Him crucified.'[16]

The stage of illumination has its peak-points in particular moments or periods when God reveals Himself in great beauty and power to the soul. It answers to the gazing *upon* God experience of the last chapter. It may be a dramatic moment of conversion such as Saul of Tarsus experienced on the Damascus road; a leaving of the nets at the shores of Galilee to follow Jesus; a turning of one's back on the piles of tax-money when Matthew heard the words 'follow me'.[17] There are also moments of revelation as when Simon Peter made his great confession at Caesarea Philippi, or when John, sitting in the boat gazing across the mists of the lake in the early morning after the resurrection, whispered to Peter in wonder: 'It is the Lord.' Then there are moments of heartfelt emotion as Mary Magdalene experienced when she had wept to the supposed gardener, and Jesus had answered: 'Mary!'[18]

As the believer grows in love and longing, the glimpses of unitive vision get stronger, and the pain of purgation sharper, but all within the life of illumination. St John of the Cross says that there is weariness of heart as long as the believer does not truly possess that which it loves. He is like a hungry man longing for food, an invalid sighing for health, or one who is suspended in the air with no firm foothold.[19]

He also emphasizes a certain passivity about the embraces

of God, for the spirit feels itself to be deeply and passionately in love with God. This love is infused into the passive soul in the sense that the believer himself cannot generate it. All the soul can do is to give itself up to the interior movements of God with great joy and increasing longing. The soul gives consent; the warmth, strength, temper and enkindling of love belong to God who is drawing the soul into union with Himself.[20] The consequence of all this is that as God wounds the soul with the interior touches of His love, the soul's longings and yearnings become more unified in God, and more withdrawn from the world-system which is involved in the illusory quest for money, ambition and power. The believer does not become vaguely other-worldly in a negative sense, but more sensitive to truth, justice and integrity. The positive qualities of people like Martin Luther King, Thomas Merton, Mother Theresa of Calcutta, indicate a life of prayer which reveals flashes of intuitive illumination and union with God. Certainly in the contemplative tradition the genuine mystics like the Carmelites St Theresa and St John of the Cross were indefatigable workers and organizers, and yet they not only reach the borderland between the illuminative vision and the unitive life, but they actually enter the promised land.

Union

This brings us to the third stage in the classic mystical path – the stage beyond purgation and illumination – the life of union in which the soul is so closely united to God that separatedness gives way to unitive vision. This is not a version of pantheism or identity-loss. There is a loss of individualism but not of the person. The reverse is true, because true personhood is now discovered by experience, and there is a deeper awareness of the co-respondence and co-relation of all things in God. The brokenness and disintegration of our fragmented humanity is healed, and the words of John Donne that no man is an island at last become true in experience. In the life of union God has replaced the pseudo-ego, the soul lives in God and God lives in the soul. This is a genuine mutual indwelling, and the *imago Dei*, the image of God, is made anew.

Epektesis

To speak of the fullnes of the unitive life is a paradoxical use of words, for although we see this fullness manifested in the life of Jesus in the Gospels and its reflection in those who are nearest to Him, for us finite creatures there is an eternal growth into the fullness. The Greek fathers called the experience *epektesis*, and a contemporary Cistercian writer expounds the teaching of Gregory of Nyssa on the subject:

> The idea of epektesis is that the perfect spiritual man is not one who has 'arrived' at a high degree of moral perfection and contemplative knowledge of God. Rather, he is the man who, having attained a high measure presses on in pursuit of still purer, more vital experience of God's light and truth. The perfect man is the man who is ever moving forward, deeper into the mystery of God. Heaven itself, in this view, consists in an eternal progress into the love and light and life of God, where each fulfilment contains in itself the impulse to further exploration.[21]

The Apostle Paul could write that he was crucified with Christ, that he lived no longer, but that the life he lived was the very life of Jesus manifested in his mortal body. On the other hand he maintained that he was longing to enter into fullness, that he had not yet descended into the depths of Christ's suffering or entered into the heights of his glory, but pressed on in anticipation of the transformation from glory to glory in the heavenly life.[22]

The paradox is obvious, and paradox it must be. We have emphasized that like the other two stages, the stage of union is both a present possession and an anticipated longing. There are moments and glimpses of the experience of union in conversion, in charisms of the

Holy Spirit, in sacramental and charismatic practices, and in all the creative and aesthetic aspects of a full, human life. When relationships are wholesome, loving and compassionate the life of union with God is anticipated most profoundly, and in the call of God into the solitude of prayer one is drawn into periods of unitive experience. But instead of satisfying the hunger, assuaging the thirst, such experiences, glimpses and periods serve only to inflame the desire for the Beloved. Among all the analogies used by the great teachers of prayer, there is a recurring use of the lover-beloved analogy. In the poetry and commentaries of St John of the Cross the lover is smitten with the wounds of love. The only one who can heal these wounds is the Beloved who inflicted them, and yet the lover would not be without them.

All the great teachers speaking of the unitive life in God come to a place where they are unable to go on. They cannot speak more of their own experiences because they realize that they are incommunicable; they cannot speak objectively of the life of union because it is beyond them, exceeding language and even thought. Both the Johannine and Pauline traditions unite in saying that it does not yet appear what we shall be, that we can only now see through a glass darkly.[23] What we can do is to share and communicate something of our glimpses and moments of union with God in Christ; we can rejoice in the truth and experience of being united to the living vine, being members of Christ's body, and temples of the Holy Spirit. But to speak of the essence of spiritual marriage is not only beyond our communicative ability, it is also beyond our present experience. There are some rare souls who live in this fruitful promised land of the unitive life, who have entered a blessed state, even on earth, that defies description and is beyond the conception of ordinary Christians. But most of us remain in the ascetical life of purgation, where our repentance opens out into the joy and delight of illumination. We may find the interior work of the Holy Spirit moving us profoundly to ever deeper experiences of union and love, up to and into dimensions of the unitive life, but by and large we groan, and long for that blessed life of seeing God face to face and entering into the fullness of participation in the trinitarian life of love.

References

1 Matt. 22:14
2 2 Tim. 2:19–22
3 2 Pet. 1:9; Heb. 1:3
4 John 15:2
5 Isa. 6:5
6 Hos. 2:16
7 Isa. 2:4
8 John 3:2; 13:30
9 Exod. 19 and 20
10 *Dark Night of the Soul*, Bk. II, ch. V.1. An excellent English Translation of the works of St John of the Cross (3 vols. in one) is: E. Allison Peers, *The Complete works of St John of the Cross*, London: (Burns and Oates, 1964)
11 *Ibid.*, Bk. II, V, 2
12 The reference here is to the experiences of patriachs and prophets like Abraham, Moses, Isaiah, Jeremiah, Ezekiel, Daniel, and especially to the outshining of the uncreated energies of God in the Transfiguration of Christ, which is the theme of the next chapter.
13 *Dark Night of the Soul*, Bk. II, V, 5; V, 7.
14 See *Ibid.*, Bk. II, X, 1
15 Rom. 6:3–6
16 1 Cor. 1:18; 2:1, 2
17 Acts 9:1–19; Matt. 4:19; Luke 5:27
18 Matt. 16:16,1; John 21:7; John 20:11–18
19 *Spiritual Canticle*, IX, V, 6,7
20 *Dark Night of the Soul*, Bk II, XI, 2
21 John Eudes Bamberger, *Continuum*, Vol. 7, No. 2., p. 238

22 Gal. 2:20; 2 Cor. 4:10,11;
    Phil. 3:10–14
23 1 John 3:2; 1 Cor. 13:12

12: Transfiguration

In our pilgrimage of prayer we have covered terrain dealing with prayer based in Scripture, expressed in personal experience, and communicated in ways of contemporary praying which have called into play areas of the physical, the psychical and the spiritual.

In this last chapter it is my intention to point to the One who is the pioneer and master on our journey, for he is the great mediator between God and men, personifying in Himself, the way, the truth and the life.[1]

There is one particular incident in the Gospels, recorded by the three synoptic writers[2] which becomes for us the model and paradigm of the life of prayer. I speak of the Transfiguration. In St Luke's Gospel it reads:

> Now about eight days after these things he took with him Peter and John and James, and went up to the mountain to pray. And as He was praying, the appearance of His countenance was altered, and His raiment became dazzling white. And behold, two men talked with Him, Moses and Elijah, who appeared in glory and spoke of His departure, which He was to accomplish at Jerusalem. Now Peter and those who were with Him were heavy with sleep but kept awake, and they saw His glory and the two men who stood with Him. And as the men were parting from Him, Peter said to Jesus, 'Master, it is well that we are here; let us make three booths, one for You and one for Moses and one for Elijah' – not knowing what he said. As he said this, a cloud came and overshadowed them, and they were afraid as they entered the cloud. And a voice came out of the

cloud, saying, 'This is my Son, my Chosen; listen to Him!' And when the voice had spoken, Jesus was found alone. And they kept silence and told no one in those days anything of what they had seen.

A few days previously, Peter had made his great confession that Jesus was truly Christ, the messiah, and Jesus had predicted his own sufferings and death. This incident of glory must be seen in the context of such a confession and prediction. We are faced with the worse that the world can do, and with the mountain-top experience of transfiguration that gives completely new perspective and the shining of Gospel hope when one descends to the valley.

If we are to follow Jesus through the Gospels in our lives of prayer, we must ascend the mountain of contemplation with Peter, James and John, and actually share in the *metamorphosis* or transformation of being which is the New Testament word rendered into English as *transfiguration*. The same verb root is used for the transformation of the renewed mind of the Christian,[3] and for 'being changed from glory to glory' as the Christian is remade in the divine image.[4]

All the mountain experiences in the life of ancient Israel were encounters with the living God: Ararat, Sinai, Carmel, Horeb, Tabor. And Christ comes to us with all the patriarchal and prophetic tradition surrounding Him as He converses on the holy mount with Moses and Elijah. This means that our deeper life of prayer is within the great company of the communion of saints who surround us as a great cloud of witnesses.[5]

We have already spoken of cosmic prayer, and here we find Jesus enveloped not only in the great spiritual tradition of the Old Testament, but in cosmic light, heavenly glory and the great cloud of the divine presence. This continues the great Exodus theme: 'And the LORD went before them by day in a pillar of cloud to lead them along the way, and by night in a pillar of fire to give them light.'[6] The very word *exodus* is the word which is used in the heavenly communion between Jesus, Moses and Elijah, for it had to do with Jesus' *departure* or *exodus* which he was to accomplish in the divine will at Jerusalem.

This transfiguration light of the mountain which shone in our Lord's body was in spiritual and physical continuity with the light and glory which transfigured the face of Moses in his mountain encounter with God, so that his face had to be veiled. But Christ's glory excels that of Moses in splendour. It is the glory that shone in the face of the proto-martyr, Stephen as, filled with the Holy Spirit, he bore witness to the power of the risen Christ.[7]

The Orthodox tradition makes much of this divine light or effulgence which is defined as the visible quality of divinity, of the energies or grace in which God makes himself known. In an illuminating chapter on the divine light, Vladimir Lossky tells the story of the 19th century Russian staretz, St Seraphim, and of his leading his friend Motovilov into an experience of the Holy Spirit manifested in the divine light. Motovilov was told by Seraphim that the true end of the Christian life is union with God in the Holy Spirit. Motovilov responds:

'All the same, I don't understand how one can be certain of being in the Spirit of God. How should I be able to recognize for certain this manifestation in myself?'

'I've already told you,' said Father Seraphim, 'that it's very simple. I've talked at length about the state of those who are in the Spirit of God; I've also explained to you how we can recognize this presence in ourselves . . . What more is necessary, my friend?'

'I must understand better everything that you have said to me.'

'My friend, we are both at this moment in the Spirit of God . . . why won't you look at me;'

'I can't look at you, Father,' I replied, 'your eyes shine like lightning; your face has become more dazzling than the sun, and it hurts my eyes to look at you.'

'Don't be afraid,' said he, 'at this very moment you've become as bright as I have. You are also at present in the fullness of the Spirit of God; otherwise, you wouldn't be able to see me as you do see me.' . . .

Encouraged by these words, I looked and was seized by holy fear. Imagine in the middle of the sun, dazzling in the brilliance of its noontide rays, the face of the man who is speaking to you. You can see the movements of his lips, the changing expression of his eyes, you can hear his voice, you can feel his hands holding you by the shoulders, but you can see neither his hands nor his body – nothing except the blaze of light which shines around with its brilliance the snow-covered meadow, and the snowflakes which continue to fall unceasingly.

'What do you feel?' asked Father Seraphim.

'An immeasurable well-being,' I replied.

'But what sort of well-being? What exactly?'

'I feel,' I replied, 'such calm, such peace in my soul, that I can find no words to express it.'

'My friend, it is the peace our Lord spoke of when he said to his disciples: ''My peace I give unto you, the peace which the world cannot give; the peace which passeth all understanding.'' What else do you feel?'

'Infinite joy in my heart.'

Father Seraphim continued: 'When the Spirit of God descends on a man, and envelops him in the fullness of His presence, the soul overflows with unspeakable joy, for the Holy Spirit fills everything He touches with joy. . . .'[8]

This is one of the many stories from the Orthodox tradition in which the light and glory of the Holy Spirit is both experienced and observed in the life of prayer. It is in clear continuity with the biblical tradition, in Moses, upon Saul on the road to Damascus, in the face of Stephen at his trial and martyrdom, and supremely on the mount of transfiguration in Jesus and those around Him. It pierced the gloom of primeval chaos when by the divine *fiat* God commanded the light to shine out of darkness. This is taken up by St Paul when he speaks of 'the light of the Gospel of the glory of Christ', and comments: 'For it is the God who said, "Let light shine out of darkness", who has shone in our hearts to give the light of the knowledge of the glory of God in the face of Christ.'[9]

On the mount of transfiguration, Jesus yielded himself to the Father in the power of the Holy Spirit, and allowed the divine and uncreated light to be manifested. What seemed supernatural to the disciples was what the writer to the Hebrews called the effulgence and glory of his very nature.[10]

Dorothy Sayers encapsulates the experience in a conversation between the three disciples during the night following the incident on the mountain. The three are whispering together on the rooftop of the house where the other disciples are asleep:

Peter: We're all right here, if we talk quietly . . . It's rather cold.

James: I have brought our cloaks . . . Look at the stars . . . Spread above the earth like a robe of glory.

Peter: But nothing to compare with the glory we saw today in the mountain.

James: No. Tell me, Simon Peter – what did you see? Was it the same for all of us?

Peter: I was tired with the climb . . . I watched him for a time as he stood and prayed, never speaking, never moving, with his face toward Jerusalem . . . as though he saw nothing but some strange inward vision that held him entranced . . . I tried to pray too, but no thoughts would come . . . It seemed to go on for ever . . .

John: As though time had stopped.

Peter: I think I lost myself a little . . . there in the silence . . . for the next thing I knew was a great terror, as though I was drowning in it – and when I looked at his face, it was not of this earth. It was . . . it was like . . . it is a thing I dare not think of . . .

James: Don't, Peter, we saw it too.

Peter: And his garments whiter than the light – the way no fuller on earth could whiten them . . .

And those two others with him . . . They spoke together but I couldn't tell what they said . . . The glory was upon them both and I knew them for blessed Moses that talked with God in Sinai, and holy Elijah who passed up to heaven in light and fire . . . and it seemed that what I saw was the reality, and the earth and the sky only a dream . . . yet I knew all the time that the sun was shining, and I could feel the rough stems of the heather between my fingers.

James: I had lost touch with everything – except John's hand in mine.

John: Dear James! – I felt you, but as though we were children again – do you remember? –

when the great thunderbolt fell, and I was frightened.

James: Oh, John – my little brother, John. It is you now that stand between me and fear.

John: I was afraid too. Peter was the bravest. He spoke.

Peter: Yes – but such nonsense! I thought the vision was departing. I remember calling out:

'Lord – it is good to be here. Can't we build three tabernacles for you and Moses and Elijah, and all stay like this for ever?' – so stupid – but I didn't know what I was saying . . . I thought of the Ark in the wilderness and the glory of the Lord in the pillar of fire . . . all mixed up somehow with the Holy City and the Feast of Tabernacles . . . And then, and then – the fire and the light were all about us . . . and the Voice . . . was it without us or within? . . . and was it a voice at all?

John: It filled everything – there was nothing in the world but the voice: 'This is My beloved Son, hear Him.'

James: And after that – nothing. Only the hills and
         the sky, and Jesus standing there alone.
Peter: He held out his hand, and I was afraid to
         touch him . . . But he was just the same . . .
as though nothing had changed in him.
John: I think the change was not in him but in us.
         I think we had seen him for a moment as he
always is . . . Perhaps the end of the world is quite
near.[11]

The three disciples represent the Church which is the
Body of Christ, and are examples of individual believers.
The glory manifested in the flesh and garments of Jesus
reflects his loving communion with the Father, and is
analogous to the indwelling Spirit which needs to be
awakened in the believer's heart. Such mystical
indwelling has been covered over by sin, materialism,
laziness, busyness and the excess of legitimate
concerns.

In the above conversation, John says. 'I think we had
seen him for a moment as he always is.' Our Lord was
always in a state of prayer and complete openness to the
Father. The disciples could also have been in such a state
of prayer, but their eyes were heavy and their hearts dull.
It is our life's work to allow the Holy Spirit to purify and
sanctify us, to cleanse the heart and cause it to beat with
the rhythm of God. When the heart is clean and open to
the indwelling Spirit with no darkening cloud between,
then the spring of prayer will bubble up. The heart, in the
biblical and monastic sense, will then pulsate with the
rhythm of God. As Paul puts it: 'When we cry "Abba!
Father!" it is the Spirit himself bearing witness with our
spirit that we are children of God.'[12] A monk who has
often lifted up in prayer to the Holy Spirit was asked how
he had reached that state. He said that he found it difficult
to explain: 'Looking back, my impression is that for
many, many years I was carrying prayer within my heart
but did not know it at the time. It was like a spring, but
one covered by a stone. Then at a certain point Jesus took

away the stone. At that the spring began to flow and has been flowing ever since.'

In this chapter we are saying that Jesus is the paradigm of our life of prayer, and that we follow him not only in the waters of our conversion and baptism and into the desert of asceticism and spiritual combat, but also up the mountain of transfiguration and glory. All the splendour and discipline of the law and the prophets will be seen in our understanding of Christ as the fulfilment of the Old Testament promises. But all else will fade into insignificance when we behold him, Jesus only, in the light of the glory that excels all other.[13]

In the account of the Transfiguration we have the life of prayer portrayed before our very eyes. The initiative is with the Father; Jesus gives himself to the prayer of vision in self-surrendered freedom and discipline; the uncreated light of the Holy Spirit floods his being and overflows into the natural order. Here is not only a penetration into the mystery of God, but an awareness of the communion of saints, the shared experience of saints on earth and in heaven. The divine presence saturates the mountain, and the voice from the excellent glory fills the disciples with awe and amazement.[14]

These are moments of wonder, of holy fear, of contemplative vision. The plain of human need stretches out below with all its opportunities and challenges to loving service. But here on the holy mount the vision encapsulates and saturates all those caught up in its glory.

Jesus carries the glory from the mount to the plain. The splendour and vision of the glory of God is translated into compassion, healing and works of mercy. Jesus, humble and transfigured, is the paradigm of the life of prayer. And we are called to follow him.

References

1 Heb. 12:2; 1 Tim. 2:5; John 14:6
2 Matt. 17:1–8; Mark 9:2–8; Luke 9:28–36

3 Rom. 12:2
4 2 Cor. 3:18
5 Heb. 12:1
6 Exod. 13:21
7 Exod. 34:29–35; 2 Cor. 3:7–18; Acts 8:55
8 Vladimir Lossky, *The Mystical Theology of the Eastern Church*, pp. 110f, London: (James Clarke, 1957).
9 Gen. 1:3; 2 Cor. 4:6
10 Heb. 1:3
11 Dorothy Sayers, *The Man Born to be King*, pp. 169f, London: Gollancz, 1943).
12 Rom. 8:15,16
13 2 Cor. 3:10
14 2 Pet. 1:16–18

Epilogue: O Let It Freely Burn

We have come to the end of our pilgrimage together, and I am aware of three things. First, I have endeavoured to share from my knowledge and experience something of the way the Lord has led me in the way of prayer. Second, I remember the ancient saying that has sounded in my heart throughout the writing of this book. 'He who speaks does not know; he who knows does not speak'. It is not that what I have shared is not valid and real for myself and for the reader, but that I am merely a beginner, paddling on the edge of that great river of God which flows from His throne. Third, I realize that I have not even told the part, either of sorrow or glory, and that there is more – so much more – flowing out into eternity.

I am filled with amazement at simply being human, at being called into communion with the mystery of God's love, and at the infinite possibilities that open out before me. These things I have sought to share in the foregoing pages.

I began with the simple stanza from one of James Montgomery's hymns. I conclude with two stanzas from the 15th century hymn to the Holy Spirit, *Discendi, Amor Santo*, by Bianco da Siena:

> O let it freely burn
>   Till earthly passions turn
> To dust and ashes in its heat consuming;
>   And let thy glorious light
>   Shine ever on my sight,
> And clothe me round, the while my path illuming.

And so the yearning strong,
   With which the soul will long,
Shall far outpass the power of human telling;
   For none can guess its grace,
   Till he become the place
Wherein the Holy Spirit makes his dwelling.

Appendix

Reflections on Solitude

What is this solitude which draws and calls me
To turn from human company and cheer,
From all the simple pleasures of companions,
From all the commerce which my friends hold dear

What is the nature of this longed-for silence,
What the attraction of these lonely days?
Joys should be shared and love communicated,
Wisdom displayed in common life and praise.

Is it perfection that I seek in secret,
Turning in sadness from a world impure?
Is disappointment mainspring of my motive
And lonely purity the source of such allure?

Or is this world the kingdom of the devil,
Lust of the flesh and eyes, and pride of life,
So that I seek the desert's stark oblivion
From sin and darkness, hatred, toil and strife?

Or do I run like those old desert fathers
In Egypt's deserts, caves of Palestine
To search far from the world for a salvation
That I can grasp and claim and hold as mine?

Or have I found a bliss and joy ecstatic,
The hidden treasure in the field of prayer
That is too precious and too high and lofty
With common souls such vision bright to share?

Or does my shrewd but coward-soul hide, lurking,
Clothed in pretence of prayer and love and faith,
While mouldering beneath such pious garments
Is the dread smell of dark decay and death?

All things most human cause me much rejoicing,
Sharing the things of earth imparts such joy;
My solitude is no aloof partaking
Of heavenly pleasures free from sin's alloy.

For the Divine delights in things most human,
The love of God is seen in loves below,
Laughter of children, sound of infant voices
Are owned by God, because He loves them so.

Nor do I turn from this vain world so tainted
To seek a secret purity and grace,
For in my own soul too the world is patterned,
Its pain is in my heart and on my face.

And if I seek salvation in the desert
Far from the crowds of sinners in the street,
There I would meet myself, oppressed and burdened,
Clasp sinful hands and walk with weary feet.

If I would flee to claim a lone salvation
Within imagined purity to dwell,
There I would find, turning from human loving
Dark alienation in an inner hell.

And if I seek to guard some joy ecstatic
Saving my treasure from corruption's rust,
Soon I would find my close-coveted treasure
Would rot away, its beauty turned to dust.

If driven by cowardice and selfish weakness
I seek the desert, there to hide away,
Phantoms of darkness, psyche's retribution
Would soon reduce my powers in disarray.

The desert has no sympathy for weakness,
Pride needs to tremble, cowardice to fear,
Only the man acknowledging transgression
Humble and contrite, may to God draw near.

Ah! there the note of truth that lures me onward,
'Tis God alone whose inward voice is heard,
And all my seeking is but a responding
Sound it so foolish or the quest absurd.

For to the desert went the Saviour, fasting,
Driven by the Spirit, and courageously
Locked and engaged in combat with the devil
Routed dark powers and gained the victory.

And in the solitude and darkness on the mountain,
Jesus spent nights of yearning and of prayer,
Caught up in glory, transported in vision,
Drawn to the Father, love divine to share.

Solitude's stillness is the place of vision,
Gazing on Beauty, wrapt in silence still,
Sharing the glory of the triune splendour
Learning the meaning of the Father's will.

There was no glory for our Saviour, Jesus,
Till He had learned the suffering of love,
And to become the bringer of salvation
Entered our darkness from His throne above.

So there is darkness, pain and isolation,
Learning to bear the beams of love divine,
Before the dawn of worship's adoration,
This was the Saviour's path, so it is mine.

Thus undistracted from the world about me,
Here in the desert I pursue my quest,
Answering the call which sounds so deep within me,
Engaged in conflict, then in love to rest.

But not alone do I pursue this vision,
The cloud of witnesses is ranged on every side,
Prayers of the church and members of Christ's body
Share in the quest, and scripture is my guide.

So having glimpsed the glory of the Eternal,
I would behold that Beauty face to face,
Till my whole being, transformed into glory,
Shall bear His likeness and reflect His grace.

Then what He wills will be, for at His bidding
I will go forth to witness to His love,
Or stay in wonder at His feet adoring,
Speak, or be still – His will divine to prove.

Construction of a Prayer Stool

You will need:
One piece of wood 14'' × 4'' × ¾''
Two pieces of wood 4'' × 6'' × ¾''
Two 3'' hinges with their screws

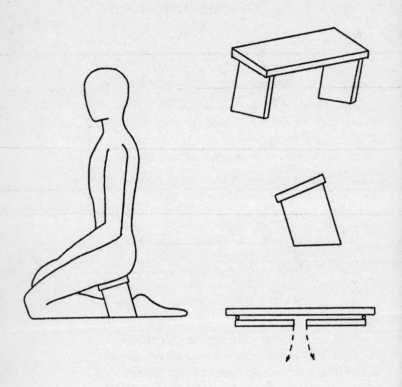

Lamb on the Anelog Mountain

Perched on the side of the Anelog mountain
On the tip of the Lleyn Peninsula
Facing the numinous Island of Bardsey
Called Ynys Enlli, Island of twenty thousand
saints,
Stands a soft, white, silent, woolly lamb.

Winter wind howls around the tiny cottage,
Mist swirls past, enveloping Anelog in clouds,
The rain is lashed by the wind,
But the lamb stands, wind-swept, wet and alone,
Looking towards my lighted window.

He does not initiate movement
But under the poor shelter of the low stone wall
Stands unsteadily, patiently, attentively,
Against the cold, wet buffeting,
Attracted by the movement and the window lamp.

Agnus Dei, qui tollis peccata mundi,
Lamb of God, by your very persistence,
By your patience, your expectation,
Your attention and concrete presence
You draw me to gaze through the window.

Miserere nobis – have mercy upon us.
Lamb of God, why do you stand so patiently
When I am so restless and uncertain?
Why do you gaze upon me so searchingly?
Is it reproach or silent yearning that you stand so?

Dona nobis pacem. The elements swirl about you,
Shrieking wind, soaking rain, and ragged mists,
Yet you stand patiently, offering me your peace,
Your silence bearing eloquent witness,
Your stillness enveloping you and me in mystery.

213

Dear lamb, why am I so immensely moved?
Why does my pulse quicken so?
Why do tears spring to my eyes?
Solitary lamb, straying on Anelog mountain,
In your presence I stand before the Lamb of
God.

Cosmic Prayer

i Unity and Harmony

1 When the frail body lays aside
Recurring, restless, active strife,
And when the mind withdraws from all
The world's demands and fretful strife,
And when the spirit's quiet and still,
There lies our peace – Your perfect will.

2 For when the body and the mind
Are in the spirit's strong control,
Disintegrated vital powers
Move towards their harmonious whole;
For body, mind and spirit move
Within the universal Love.

3 Love is the energy of life,
The fabric of the cosmic power,
And when we give ourselves to love
In every meditation hour
Its repercussion circles round
Re-echoing love's deep, mystic sound.

4 The body lives and moves and grows
Within the pattern of the whole,
Rooted in earth and sea and sky
It breathes within the cosmic soul;
God's Spirit moves within the earth
Bringing His life and love to birth.

5 The breath of God breathes through the world
Manifestation of His life;
We breath in rhythmic, glad response
Inbreathing peace, expelling strife,
Till spirit, mind and body free
Joy in such cosmic harmony.

1 The whole creation groans in pain
  Travails in birth and burdened sore;
  Its yearning felt in Autumn's shade,
  In sky's expanse and ocean's road,
  Awaiting consummation's hour –
  Christ's healing and transforming power.

2 In microscopic clarity
  Each man of prayer may hear the call
  Within the confines of the heart
  Wherein is there reflected all –
  All ecstasy, bliss and delight,
  All sorrow, pain and darkest night.

3 In Christ's redeeming, suffering love
  In which all men may share a part
  There lies the reconciling power
  With meditation's healing art
  To share in His redeeming love
  And His transfiguring passion prove.

4 The cosmic pain is finitude
  And sin's decay and passion's lust;
  Contingent powers long for release,
  Perfection's hopes lie in the dust,
  While on the dark horizon's line
  Are signs of this world's last decline.

5 So men of God are drawn to prayer
  By the indwelling Spirit's call,
  And men of faith and love arise
  Reversing thus the cosmic fall;
  Redeeming man's aridity,
  Renewing earth's fertility.

1 Jesus, the weak and mortal man
   Bowed down in dark Gethsemane
   Is cosmic Lord of life and death,
   Reigning as King from Calvary;
   And by his stripes our wounds are healed,
   And by His love our pain annealed.

2 For surely He has borne our griefs,
   Carried our sorrows in His Heart;
   We see Him stricken, and are drawn
   To share such grief, to bear our part,
   For by His wounds He brings us peace,
   And grants the captive glad release.

3 Bearing our sins as Lamb of God
   He was brought to the jaws of death,
   But in the Father's gracious will
   Was raised up by the Spirit's breath;
   We follow up that sacred stair
   Through suffering, to the life of prayer.

4 The way of prayer leads to His heart
   Filled with a universal love,
   Gazing upon our glorious Head
   Now we His healing wonders prove;
   For suffering, in His great design
   Begets a healing power divine.

5 And from His cross there radiates
   A healing light, a soothing balm
   Which shines through all created worlds
   Redeeming from malicious harm,
   Grace elevating nature's loss
   Infusing life by that same cross.

1 Christ is the Father's Son divine,
   Incarnate, slain and raised above;
   Before all worlds He stands supreme
   The cosmic Lord of life and love;
   And we, in Him, are raised from death,
   Inspired by the Spirit's breath.

2 His body, raised above all worlds
   Shines with the Godhead's glorious light,
   And in the sacramental feast
   Is given, though veiled from mortal sight;
   Made one with Him, raised from the dead,
   His members we, and He the Head.

3 The man of prayer fixes his heart
   In contemplation on his Lord;
   Body and mind and spirit held
   In stillness by the living Word,
   Thus the whole world's affected by
   His yearning heart, his burdened sigh.

4 Alone, yet in communion with
   The saints on earth and saints above,
   The mystic power of Christ the Head
   His Body fills with healing love;
   He reconciling grace bestows
   While healing balm around Him flows.

5 And in this union mystical
   Within the Fount of Deity
   The Father, Son and Spirit dwell
   Strong Trinity in Unity;
   And we are drawn such love to share
   Upon the mystic path of prayer.

Contemplation of the Cross

A dialogue between two friars

First brother
I flee the Cross that doth my heart devour
I cannot bear its ardour and its power.
I cannot bear this great and dreadful heat,
Far from the Cross, from Love on flying feet
I haste away; my heart at every beat
   Consumes me with that burning memory.

Second brother
Brother, why dost thou flee from this delight?
This is the joy I yearn for, day and night:
Brother this is but weakness in my sight,
   To flee from joy and peace so cravenly.

First brother
Brother, I flee, for I am wounded sore,
My heart is pierced and sundered to the core;
Thou hast not felt the anguish that I bore,
   Else wouldst thou speak in other words to me.

Second brother
Brother, I find the Cross all garlanded,
And with its blossoms do I wreathe my head;
It wounds me not; nay, I am comforted;
   The Cross is all delight and joy to me.

First brother
I find it full of arrows sharp, that dart
Forth from its side: they reach, they pierce my heart
The Archer aims His shafts that tear and smart;
   And through my armour He hath wounded me.

Second brother
I once was blind, but now I see the light;
Gazing upon the Cross I found my sight.
Beneath the Cross my soul is glad and bright;
   Far from the Cross I am in misery.

First brother

Not so with me: this Light hath made me blind!
So fierce the lustre that around me shined,
My head is giddy, and confused my mind,
   Mine eyes are dazzled that I cannot see.

Second brother

Now can I speak, I that was once so dumb;
'Tis from the Cross that all my powers come;
Yea, by that Cross, of Thought and Love the Sum,
   Now I can preach to men full potently.

First brother

The Cross hath made me dumb, who spoke so well;
In such a deep abyss my heart doth dwell,
I cannot speak, and nothing can I tell;
   And none can understand nor talk with me.

Second brother

Lo, I was dead, and now new life is mine,
Life that was given me by the Cross divine;
Yea, parted from the Cross, in death I pine,
   Its Presence gives me all vitality.

First brother

I am not dead, but dying day by day,
Would God that I were dead and passed away!
Eternally I struggle, gasp, and pray,
   And nothing that I do can set me free.

Second brother

Brother, to me the Cross is all delight;
Beneath it dwells no torment nor affright:
Perchance thou hast not felt that Union's might,
   Nor that Embrace, that clasps so tenderly.

First brother

Ah, thou art warmed; but I am in the Fire:
Thine the delight, and mine the flaming Pyre;
I cannot breathe within this furnace dire!
   Thou hast not entered There, It burns not thee.

Second brother
Brother, thy words I cannot understand:
Why dost thou flee from gentle Love's demand?
Tell me thy state, and let me take thy hand,
   The while I listen to this mystery!

First brother
Brother, thou breath'st the perfume of the Wine;
But I have drunk It, and no strength of mine
Can bear the onslaught of that Must Divine,
   That ruthless, ceaseth not to torture me!

Jacapone da Todi, 1228–1306

If you wish to receive *regular information* about *new books,* please send your name and address to:

London Bible Warehouse
PO Box 123
Basingstoke
Hants RG23 7NL

Name ....

Address ....

....

....

....

I am especially interested in:
☐ Biographies
☐ Fiction
☐ Christian living
☐ Issue related books
☐ Academic books
☐ Bible study aids
☐ Children's books
☐ Music
☐ Other subjects